Louder
than
Words

Louder than Words

THE ART OF LIVING
AS A CATHOLIC

BY

MATTHEW LEONARD

OUR SUNDAY VISITOR PUBLISHING DIVISION
OUR SUNDAY VISITOR, INC.
HUNTINGTON, INDIANA 46750

ISBN: 978-1-61278-627-8 (Inventory No. T1324)
eISBN: 978-1-61278-290-4
LCCN: 2012955319

Cover design: Lindsey Riesen
Cover art: Shutterstock
Interior design: Dianne Nelson

PRINTED IN THE UNITED STATES OF AMERICA

DEDICATION

To my loving wife, Veronica

TABLE OF CONTENTS

FOREWORD
by Mike Aquilina

"MAGNANIMITY" IS NOT A WORD I USE VERY OFTEN.

It's not a word I can pronounce very easily. But it comes to my mind when I think of Matthew Leonard.

Matt's an old friend. He has many longtime friends because he makes us laugh hysterically — and because he's demanding of us. Matt looks at people and sees not what they see when they look in the mirror, but what God must see when he makes them. Matt sees what we *could* do, if we really wanted to, and then he starts nudging us in the direction of doing it.

That brings me back to the big word. "Magnanimity" comes from the Latin *magna* and *anima* — "great" and "soul." Magnanimity is greatness of soul, and it's something we're all supposed to have.

Magnanimity is holy ambition. It's the desire to do great things for God — and not just the desire, but the active, habitual pursuit of those great things. God did not call us to adequacy, but to sainthood. Jesus said: "You, therefore, must be perfect, as your heavenly Father is perfect" (Mt 5:48). That's a hard saying for me because I have a tough enough time with adequacy. But I can't find a loophole anywhere in the Lord's summons.

It's not that I haven't tried. My usual response to people like Jesus and Matt Leonard is phony humility: "You don't mean little old me. I'm a slug. I am not worthy. I'll give you the phone number of someone who can do it better. Why don't you call my wife?"

Whether or not we have the strength or the smarts is beside the point. If Jesus issues the call, he's going to provide the means. Saint Paul had no illusions about his abilities, but he had magnanimity: "I can do all things in him who strengthens me" (Phil 4:13).

Saint Thomas Aquinas put it in more bracing terms: "If one disdains glory in such a manner that he makes no effort to do that which merits glory, that action is blameworthy."

Matt Leonard wants to wake us up to the fact of God's power, which has been coursing through us since the day of our baptism. Matt Leonard wants to take us back to the Scriptures and show us that God repeatedly chooses weak folks like us to accomplish glorious things. David is the least impressive of a great clan of brothers, yet he's the one who becomes the greatest king in all history. Moses is a lousy orator, yet he becomes history's great lawgiver. Peter's just a mess in so many ways, yet Our Lord declares him to be The Rock on which the unshakable and everlasting Church will be built!

We write history our way, and God writes it his way. We judge some people up to the task, and others not. We think history turns on the decisions of generals and the advance of armies. God knows that it's far more likely to turn on a grandparent's kindness shown in some small way, unremarked in The Associated Press and even on Facebook. But that kindness will arise from the soul of a grandparent who is ready, willing, and prepared to be a Moses or David, if God should call for it.

When we read what's written in the Book of Life we'll be in for some surprises. We don't want to be in for blame, so we should listen up when Matt Leonard is talking to us, and take notes, and take action. Even as he makes us laugh, he's urging us to magnanimity — greatness of soul — and holy ambition. Like Jesus, he wants us to be saints, to be perfect.

Life is too short for the cowardice of false humility. Let the words of this book ring loudly in your heart. May they echo in your prayers. And may those words, like the love of Christ, urge us on — compel us — to action.

CHAPTER 1

NO REGRETS

I WAS STANDING IN FRONT OF MY TELEVISION one evening giving my thumb a vigorous workout with the remote, when I happened across one of those inane shows that focus ridiculous amounts of attention on celebrities. Normally, I would have continued my channel surfing with reckless abandon, but I paused because the person being interviewed was the iconic Andy Griffith.

I'm not old enough to have watched *The Andy Griffith Show* in prime time. In fact, I only learned to whistle the show's infectious theme song from afternoon reruns. But I'd seen enough about Andy over the years to develop a healthy respect for him as a man. I knew "America's Sheriff" to be a wholesome role model, a Christian man in Hollywood who wasn't afraid to speak of his faith. He wasn't perfect, to be sure, but to my mind he was a success in many ways and deserved any attention he got. That's why what he said stopped me cold.

The occasion for the interview was his eightieth birthday. After celebrating his long life and listing his impressive career achievements, the interviewer posed the obligatory question we've heard countless times. "If you could change anything about your life," she asked, "what would it be?" In a matter-of-fact tone he immediately responded, "Everything."

Everything? The reporter was as stunned as I was. Usually people say they wouldn't change anything because they cherish all the experiences they've had. "They've made me who I am" is the typical conclusion. Yet here was a man who had garnered money and fame, and respect from all quarters, but given the chance he would change every bit of it. Why? Because as a Christian in the twilight of his life, he explained, he knew he had left much undone. He could have made himself much more useful to God.

Odd as it seems, this celebrity gossip show was a watershed moment in my life. Andy's statement instantly challenged my priorities and made me ponder what was most important in this life. It filled me with a fear of one day having regrets about wasting the precious time I've been given on this earth.

And just so you know, it wasn't as if I was out holding up convenience stores or stealing old ladies' purses. I definitely considered myself a faithful Catholic who was trying hard as a husband and father to provide materially and spiritually for my family. I even taught Bible studies at my local parish. Wasn't that enough? Nope. As I've come to realize, there's more — a lot more. French author Leon Bloy nailed it when he said that "life holds only one tragedy: not to have been a saint."

Temper, Temper

Think about that for a moment. We're all familiar with the concept of sainthood, but it's easy to forget that saints were real people. They lived real lives that involved far more than the highlights we read in their biographies. They struggled with temptation and vice just like us. Except for Mary, saints were never sinless.

Take a guy like Saint Jerome. He may have been one of the greatest Scripture scholars of all time, but he was still a crank. Jerome was intense and passionate — few were safe from his poisonous pen when he lost patience or was running low on charity. The man who spent a good portion of his life translating the Old Testament into Latin was a grouch of biblical proportions. As poet Phyllis McGinley put it:

"God's angry man, His crotchety scholar, /
was Saint Jerome, / the great name-caller, /
who cared not a dime / for the laws of libel /
and in his spare time / translated the Bible."[1]

Jerome probably wasn't a guy you'd want to hang out with on the weekend. Even so, he loved God deeply and overcame his shortcomings through grace to become a great saint and Doctor of the Church.

Of course, Jerome wasn't the only saint capable of a tantrum. Saint Vincent de Paul's emotional explosions are almost as well-known as the incredible work he did. This French priest, whose name instantly conjures up images of ministry to the poor, besought God to help tame his angry outbursts.

> I addressed myself to Our Lord, and I earnestly begged Him to change my austere and disagreeable disposition.... And by the grace of Our Lord, together with a little care, I have succeeded in repressing the impulses of nature, and I have thereby rid myself to a certain extent of my ill temper.[2]

That's the thing about the saints. They were regular people who sought superhuman grace to overcome their frailties. Wanting to be holy more than anything else, they faced great challenges and prevailed through God's help. The saints are proof positive of Saint Paul's declaration that "I can do all things in him who strengthens me" (Phil 4:13).

I can accept that saints were just like me, but I have to chuckle at the thought of my mug on a laminated holy card. It's almost too ludicrous to imagine. Yet isn't that the goal? Not to have your image immortalized on a bookmark, but to be a saint. Many others have done it, and we're supposed to as well. Jesus himself tells us to "be perfect, as your heavenly Father is perfect" (Mt 5:48).

That's a pretty shocking statement. Every single one of us is called to perfection. Talk about a high bar! Is Jesus exaggerating? Isn't that impossible for everyone descended from Adam and Eve? Apparently not. Jesus also tells us that "with God all things are possible" (Mt 19:26). In fact, the point of Christ's incarnation, death and resurrection is to help us toward perfection so that we might join his divine family and the communion of saints in heaven.

One (Really) Big Happy Family

Perfection may not happen until we're finally united with God, but eternity isn't something that begins after we die. Once born, every one of us is an immortal being with an eternal destiny. Baptism was our first taste of God's life, instilling supernatural grace into our souls. But the process of perfection continues until the day we enter the heavenly courts, a spiritual maturation that mimics our physical growth from infancy to adulthood.

Although perfection can happen only through God's power, we have a part to play. Our main job? To get rid of whatever keeps his grace from having its maximum impact on our life as it brings us to spiritual maturity.

But here's the kicker: it's not enough to progress personally. We're supposed to help others toward perfection, too. (It turns out that we actually are our brother's keeper.) This is how we fulfill the whole law: loving God with all our heart and loving our neighbor as ourselves (see Mt 22:36-40). We're all part of the same human family that God desires to save and make a part of his divine family (1 Tm 2:4, Gal 3:28), because at the end of the day, that's what the Church is — God's family.

This truth struck me deeply at the Easter Vigil in 1998 when I was received into the Catholic Church. There I was, packed like a sardine into the front row of the field house at Franciscan University of Steubenville. Years of study, prayer, and tears had come down to this night, and I had to keep reminding myself it was really happening. I was actually becoming (gulp) a Catholic.

As I was the son of a Protestant pastor, my odyssey into the Catholic Church had caused great upheaval. Most of my friends and family could not fathom why I had chosen to become a "papist," and a painful gulf had developed between us. My wonderful new friends at the university salved my wounds with their kindness and generosity, but I grieved over the spiritual chasm that now separated me from my family. Not that it was any easier for them. While a few of my relatives did their best to support me, my conversion was difficult for all.

In spite of this spiritual estrangement from my family, when it finally came time for holy Communion, I couldn't wait to receive Our Lord. One of my sponsors said I actually elbowed him out of the way to get to the front of the line. Even if I did inflict bodily damage, can you blame me? After all, I was about to encounter God in a radically new way. The whole thing was surreal.

After returning to my seat and thanking the Lord for all he had done to push me — at times kicking and screaming — into the Catholic Church, I started looking around. It was hard not to. There were thousands of people filing past me to receive the same God I had. And that's when it hit me. These people, most of whom I had never met, had become my family in a way that transcended blood relations. They certainly didn't replace my parents and siblings. No one could ever do that. But I realized I had become a part of the family of God in a new and deeper way through the sacraments. Suddenly, I didn't feel quite so alone. This was the biggest family reunion I had ever attended!

Of course, being part of a family comes with responsibility. Just as parents ecourage their children to look out for and take care of each other, so too are we to watch out for our brothers and sisters in Christ. You and I have a responsibility to push ourselves and each other to heights of holiness, to our final home in heaven.

But as children in God's family, we have an added role. Our Father wants us to help him expand the family. There are plenty of places at his table, and he asks us to invite the whole neighborhood over for dinner. In fact, he wants them to move in and stay forever, like a perpetual sleepover.

May I Have Your Attention, Please?

In truth, some of us have tried to bring others to the table, attempting to evangelize family, friends, or even strangers. More often than not, we come up empty. Why? Among other reasons, it's hard to talk with people who won't listen longer than politeness demands (which isn't very long these days). Everybody is busy with this, that, and the other — we're consumed with created things instead of the Creator. I have to confess that at times I'm as guilty as the next guy, easily distracted by the world. After all,

God made some pretty cool stuff for our enjoyment. Even he said it was all "very good" back in the Book of Genesis (1:31). The problem is that all too often the pleasures of this world have our full attention. For most people there's no room for anything else.

This is the difficult situation in which Christianity now finds itself. The things of God are not anywhere near the top of most people's lists. Remember when it was taboo to discuss religion and politics at parties for fear of offending somebody? Better to keep your mouth shut about God and the president; stick to work and children. That's not always the case any longer. While politics is more divisive than ever, religion has been put on the back burner by too many people. Our passions seem to lie elsewhere. (Say "Notre Dame" and most people immediately think "football," not "Our Lady.") Instead of being a point of contention, religion has turned into something all too often ignored or even mocked. Unlike ages past, nobody is getting into fistfights over doctrine.

How did our faith become so irrelevant to so many people? How did we lose the ability to get society to turn, take notice, and follow us? As hard as it is to imagine, this Church — which boasts a billion members — has lost its place as the primary influence on the world. Even more incredibly, we've lost it to people who have never experienced the breathtaking grace and truth of Jesus Christ. They're stuck in the mire of sin, yet they're the ones setting the agendas and dictating the culture. It's more than a little disturbing.

I think a good portion of the problem is that Christians today tend to blend in more than stand out. We look like everyone else. We talk like everyone else. We live like everyone else. We're so assimilated that there's not much left to make us, or our message, very distinctive. So why should people stop and pay attention?

Don't get me wrong. I'm not saying we should go around picking fistfights or making spectacles of ourselves, or being different for the sake of being different. I'm talking about living saintly lives of virtue and holiness that can't help but be noticed.

Perhaps right now you're thinking to yourself, "Did he just say 'saintly' again? *Sheesh!* I have a hard time being 'goodly' much less like one of those people in a saints' book." If that's what you're thinking, then fine, welcome to my world. But you know what? As we've already seen, saints were pretty normal people. They lived in the same world we do; they just weren't of it.

Give Me More!

If Saint Thomas More, for example, stood in a police lineup with a bunch of other men with funny hats and velvet robes, you couldn't immediately tag him as the super-holy guy. Except for the sixteenth-century wardrobe, More was like a lot of other gentlemen you might know. He was well-educated, happily married with kids, and he had a good job. (He was the Lord High Chancellor of England — think good Darth Vader with a cool accent.)

While More looked like his contemporaries, he was quite different from most because, rooted in virtue and a passionate love of God, he lived according to a higher, holy standard in every aspect of his life. A lawyer by trade, More would work to persuade his clients to settle out of court because that would be cheaper. (Demons everywhere are purchasing ice skates.) And if his client was dead set on litigation, he would guide them in the most cost-effective path.[3] (If you think he won't charge you fifteen minutes for opening the package, perhaps you can send a copy of More's biography to your lawyer.) Regardless, I think you'd agree with me that this saintly attorney didn't just pass the bar; he raised it.

No Nunsense

Come to think of it, except for the "man" part, the "Lord High Chancellor" part, and the fact that he was beheaded (did I fail to mention that?), Thomas More reminds me a bit of Elizabeth Ann Seton. Both were saints, well-educated, and had a family — Elizabeth Ann had five children. One of her grandkids even became an archbishop.[4] But unlike the rest of us, at the same time she was raising her kids she founded a religious order, opened the first American parish school, and started the first Catholic orphanage in the United States. We are talking about one serious multitasker.

Mother Seton and Thomas More were firmly rooted in this world; raising their children, working their jobs, engaging the culture — in short, living life. But both knew that they were laborers in the King's vineyard. And this knowledge affected the manner in which they carried out their everyday duties. Neither of them was a mystic or had any extraordinary spiritual gifts, but they both shared one important trait: loving abandonment to God. They gave their lives unconditionally to their Father in heaven, seeking to be like his Son through the power of the Holy Spirit. They relied upon him to help them through life and trusted him completely, knowing that "all things work for good for those who love God, who are called according to his purpose" (Rom 8:28, NAB). Simply by striving for holiness on a daily basis, they became huge, blinking neon signs that pointed to Jesus. The world couldn't help but take notice.

Are You Ready?

So what's the point? Simply this. If there's one thing that Thomas More, Elizabeth Ann Seton, Vincent de Paul, and a multitude of others have taught us, it's that becoming a saint is the best way to lead others to Christ. (Even better than bingo!) Holiness is the bonfire that draws people in from the cold, dark night of sin. Our lives must radiate the power of Christ's grace and the warmth of his love. This is the foundation of our faith, the "initial act of evangelization" according to Pope Paul VI.[5]

If we're taking our faith even half-seriously, the question that we all eventually confront is, "Are you ready?"

Are you ready to follow the examples of the holy men and women who have come before us? Are you ready to "leave it all out on the field!" as my football coach used to yell? Of course, he also screamed things like, "Hit them so hard the snot shoots out of their nose!" Regardless of his many rhetorical shortcomings, his question in this case is worth asking. Are you ready to leave it all out on the field, to give all you've got for God so that you exit this life a saint? He's waiting for you. In fact, he's longing for you, desperately hoping you'll be willing to live your life totally for him.

If you've come to this place in life and you're still on the fence, I want to remind you of something: God made you. You wouldn't even exist were it not for his unfathomable love. As your Creator, he knows what makes you tick and what is going to make you most happy. In fact, he's got big plans for you, plans to bless you, "to give you a future and a hope," says the prophet Jeremiah (Jer 29:11). All you have to do is say "yes," and he'll fulfill you in ways that nothing and nobody else can. He'll even use your "yes" to bring hope and salvation to the rest of the world. In other words, you'll be as happy and fulfilled as possible and will help lead others to happiness and fulfillment, too. Does it get any better than that?

CHAPTER 2

SPRINGING INTO ACTION

I'M NOT GOING TO LIE. This book is a bit dangerous and might make you uncomfortable. It certainly makes me uncomfortable because it applies as much to my life as yours. At some point in these pages both of us may find ourselves challenged to make substantial changes in our lives, changes that can be difficult, especially at first.

On the other hand, if you take the message of this book to heart, I promise that you will discover a newfound peace, joy, and purpose unlike anything this world offers. You will become a channel of grace and an instrument of salvation. A fire of love will be lit in your soul that makes everything else pale in comparison — and there is no time to waste.

We live at a turning point in history. There is no doubt that the twentieth century had its highs and lows. It gave us the Second Vatican Council, but two world wars. We put a man on the moon, but endured the constant threat of nuclear holocaust. Tragically, the baby boom was soon followed by the scourge of abortion.

To be sure, society has needed a fresh infusion of the Gospel message for a long time. Responding to the crisis almost four decades ago, Pope Paul VI sounded the alarm for the need for a "new period of evangelization" in the world.[6] In his 1975 apostolic exhortation *Evangelii Nuntiandi* (on evangelization in the modern world), he proclaimed that the Church "exists in order to evangelize" and that the time had come to reenergize and reengage a world that had become critically ill. It is a mission, he said, that "the vast and profound changes of present-day society make all the more urgent" (14).

In other words, humanity had become a world full of prodigal sons who needed to return to their Father's home. It was time to show them the way. Of course, we know the remaining years of the twentieth century were no cakewalk. Not many were listening. The alarm had gone off, but the building was still on fire.

Flower Children

It was thus with a welcome sigh of relief that Catholics greeted Pope Blessed John Paul II's call for a "springtime of evangelization" at the dawn of the third millennium. New to the Church, I partook of the giddy delight of my fellow theology students in graduate school. Many of us believed it was the dawn of a new age. Winter was over. Spring was here. With the wind at our back and the sun high in the sky we would skip through the daisies gathering lost souls.

The decade that followed these heady days made it clear we didn't have a clue. As can be true in the natural order, our springtime weather seemed nastier than the winter. Vocations were scarce. Scandal rocked the Church. People lost their faith. Those who remained often didn't understand, much less follow, Church teaching. Large portions of our culture seemed to be devolving into ever more shocking and brazen displays of wickedness.

And yet there were (and are) many holy Catholics who faithfully continued to work and pray, secure in the knowledge that this, too, shall pass. But many of us were still asking: "Was this springtime? Was this the New Evangelization?" It appeared that something wasn't working.

Part of our problem was the naive idealism of youth. (If you're asking yourself what that means, it probably still applies to you.) We didn't yet understand what the pope had in mind, and I think the problem persists today. Many of us lack a full understanding of evangelization. What exactly is it?

The term itself comes from the Latin word for "Gospel," *evangelium*. It's the "good news" of salvation through Jesus Christ. In a nutshell, to evangelize means to teach people "the art of living" so as to lead them to life and happiness in Christ.[7] But the Gospel is not just a proclamation about Jesus; it is Jesus himself. It's an encounter with a divine person, an encounter that changes the way we speak and act and live. It changes everything.

Unfortunately, many people confuse the New Evangelization" with programs or committees. For others, it conjures up images of uncomfortable encounters with a proselytizing stranger at the door, or with members of evangelical Protestant denominations. But the New Evangelization is not a published document. It's not something you can sit in on at your local parish. Nor is it a market that's been cornered by our separated brethren. Rather, it is a re-proposing of the "perennial truth of Christ's Gospel," as Pope Benedict XVI proclaimed.[8] It's an ongoing process that Blessed John Paul II called the "primary service which the Church can render to every individual and to all humanity."[9] And it begins with you.

Can I Get a Witness?

A Christian life is supposed to be a proclamation of Jesus Christ, not just in words, but in action. Put simply, people should meet Christ when they meet a Christian. We are his face to the world. And one of the emphatic declarations made by Paul VI was that "above all the Gospel must be proclaimed by witness."[10] In other words, we need people who are actually striving after God on a daily basis. They are the true evangelizers. Indeed, "modern man listens more willingly to witnesses than to teachers, and if he does listen to teachers, it is because they are witnesses," declared the pope.[11]

Shortly after becoming Catholic, I had the opportunity to stand only a few feet away from John Paul II at a Wednesday audience in Rome. It was for only a few brief moments, but I'll never forget the aura of his presence.

Despite his obvious frailty, there was something incredibly powerful about this man. He radiated holiness and love. You couldn't help but be affected. He so moved me that I remained in the open when large storm clouds came rolling in over Saint Peter's Square right before his final blessing. Most fled for the protection of the colonnades as cold raindrops fell like small grenades out of the darkened sky, but I couldn't leave. I wanted to stand with him. I wanted his blessing. This man loved God, and I knew he loved me, too. And I'm not the only one.

The whole world paid attention to the pope because he was real — you couldn't ignore his authenticity. He practiced what he preached, and he preached what he practiced. The twinkle in his eye and the fire in his heart drew us to him. We all hung on his words. In his later years he bore his many infirmities with grace and humility, and his ability to inspire us only grew stronger.

In fact, if we had been paying more attention, the Holy Father was showing us the true path of the New Evangelization. He was living it for the world to see. It wasn't just a catchphrase. No matter the difficulties encountered, he was a witness to hope. He was a witness to love. He was a witness to holiness.

The stakes of this life are so high that we *must* strive for sainthood and embrace extreme holiness. John Paul II declared that "today we have the greatest need of saints whom we must assiduously beg God to raise up."[12] Why? Because saints are game-changers.

The pope not only prayed for it; he delivered it. And one of the things that I especially loved was that he had fun doing it. He truly enjoyed pointing others to Christ and was incredibly savvy about how he went about it. Remember when he put on rock star Bono's signature sunglasses? The pope traded a rosary for perhaps the most recognizable shades in the world and turned it into an evangelistic home run. It was the headline image everywhere. The U2 front man was completely taken by his charm, as was the rest of the planet. That little display of humor affected the way everyone thought about the papacy, the Church, and Jesus Christ.

Seriously Funny

If a pope in sunglasses caused that many heads to turn, imagine the effect a guy like Saint Philip Neri must have had. A quick look at his life reveals a man who was serious about God, but he refrained from taking himself too seriously. In fact, he was hilarious. He cracked me up enough that when I was preparing to enter the Church I considered taking Philip as my confirmation name. (Instead, I chose James, because that book of the Bible always provides a needed kick in the pants.)

Like John Paul II, Philip Neri destroys the image of saints as an austere bunch that piously moves from place to place, perpetually chanting. He was kind of a goofball for Christ who was known as much for his humor as his holiness.

When I first I heard about this intriguing man who went about, at times, with half his beard shaved off, I smiled. When I read about the time he repeatedly tugged on the beard of one of the pope's Swiss guards in front of a large crowd, I chuckled. (Facial hair was apparently a frequent target.) But I broke out laughing when I came across what one biographer wrote about Saint Philip: "Sometimes he went down into the church on a great feast, with a jacket on inside out over his cassock, and his beretta [sic] cocked on one side, followed by one of the community with a brush who kept brushing him before all the people."[13]

In fact, when this pious saint entertained distinguished guests, he would sometimes make them wait within earshot while he had joke books read to him, all the while pretending the stories were of the greatest importance to him. His visitors had come to see a holy sage, but often left shaking their heads and wondering at his oddities.

"Okay," you're thinking, "this guy was funny and kept things light, but I would be absolutely mortified by this kind of behavior." Saint Philip's response to you would be, "Exactly!" He didn't engage in silly antics simply because he liked a little levity now and then. He did it because he hoped his seeming silliness would take people's eyes off him. He didn't want the attention.

Philip's reputation for sanctity left many people in awe of him — too many, as far as Philip was concerned. He wanted people to stop putting him on a pedestal and get their eyes back on Christ. He mortified himself, making himself out to be a fool, so that pride wouldn't take root and cause him to get too big for his britches (or whatever he wore). That's why he would sometimes do ridiculous things. His humor had a serious goal for himself and others: heaven.

Our Turn

While in some ways Saint Philip Neri was one of a kind, his story is not singular. Beginning with the apostles, Church history is teeming with stories of men and women who have made God the center of their lives. Through their witness the faith has spread to the corners of the earth. More than one billion people now identify themselves as Catholic, many millions more as Christians of one stripe or another.

Even so, most of the world remains in need of conversion, and there is no shortage of work to be done. You and I need to pick up where people like Thomas More, Mother Seton, and Philip Neri left off. Their lives, like those of so many other giants of the faith, are a blueprint not only for the art of living, but for successful evangelization as well. They have shown us the way. We might not be founding religious orders or pulling people's beards, but we're called to the same degree of sanctity that these saints achieved.

In case you're thinking, "There's no way I could ever reach those heights of holiness," remember that the saints didn't suddenly acquire saintliness. Saints are made, not born. Their death was the final consummation of a life joined to Christ every day, a life of faith and virtue that led to salvation for them and others. We're called to the same.

Follow the Leader

The Church's call for a New Evangelization provides a mandate, a goal, for the life of every Catholic. It doesn't matter if you're a priest, religious, banker, fireman, or store clerk; the call is universal. And regardless of the evangelistic activity in which you may be involved, the starting point is always you, your personal life. To evangelize effectively you must first be evangelized. You have to draw close to God and become an example. The things we say, the things we do — everything about us — should cause others to look to the One in whom "we live and move and have our being" (Acts 17:28).

And rather than delay, we need to be on the offense. We can't wait for the world to come to Christ; we have to take Christ to the world. Jesus didn't ask his apostles to sit around. He sent them out! "*Go* ... and make disciples of all nations" (Mt 28:19, emphasis mine). The early Church continued his example as did those who followed through the centuries. Now it's our turn. We are now those "others" Christ is empowering to go out into the whole world and preach the Gospel (see Mk 16:15).

Don't forget that Jesus never works alone. He invites you to share in his magnificent labor of love and its rewards. He has a special role for you, a part for you to play in this drama of salvation, and all you have to do is say "yes."

CHAPTER 3

WHAT'S SO NEW ABOUT EVANGELIZATION?

SOMETIMES I FEEL A BIT COWED by the task in front of us. I'd be lying if I said otherwise. But imagine if you were one of the apostles, the very first evangelizers of the Church. Unlike us they weren't re-evangelizing, but spreading a new Gospel message in the face of incredible odds. After a few days of hiding out, wondering what exactly was going to happen after the death and resurrection of Jesus, they caught fire (almost literally) and proclaimed the faith to all who would listen.

Like a rocket blasting off from its launchpad toward the heavens, they were in stage one. While Saint Peter was mission control, Saint Paul was the lead astronaut. Boldly going where no Christian man had gone before, Paul spread the faith everywhere, particularly among the Gentiles. He braved angry mobs, shipwrecks, snakes, and much more in his quest to bring others to the joy he had found in Christ.

Of course, Paul and the apostles were followed by countless others over the centuries who dedicated their lives to proclaiming salvation through Jesus. But now we've arrived at a moment when a New Evangelization is needed, specifically a renewal of the faith of people who have heard of Christ, and perhaps once practiced the faith, but who no longer live for him.

Small Is Beautiful

Almost an entire generation has passed since Paul VI first issued his call for renewal. While many people have responded, the problems facing us are more acute than ever. Measured by worldly statistics and scientific "metrics," we seem to be losing, and this can lead to despair and withdrawal. In response to this dilemma, Pope Benedict XVI, when still Cardinal Joseph Ratzinger, reminded us of the parable of the mustard seed. He warned against impatience and focusing on quickly attracting large numbers to the faith. "Exterior power is not the sign of his presence," he said.[14] Rather, "new evangelization ... means to dare, once again and with the humility of the small grain, to leave up to God the when and how it will grow."[15]

This was certainly the case with Saint Thérèse of Lisieux, the Little Flower. When her mother superior (who was in fact her sister) ordered her to write down her childhood memories, nobody had any idea it would lead to one of the greatest books on spirituality ever written. Some of her fellow Carmelites thought *The Story of a Soul*, as it came to be known, was nothing more than a source from which they could compile her obituary after it became apparent she would soon die of tuberculosis.[16]

The legacy of Saint Thérèse doesn't include the typical trappings of evangelistic success such as rallies at football stadiums or missionary travel to distant lands. Hers was the "little way." She sought to please God and grow in holiness through the ordinary activity of life. Whatever she did, she did for God.

It's not that she didn't want to do great things — in fact, she originally wanted to be a missionary — but she realized early on that her success would come in a different form. In *The Story of a Soul* she speaks of her fascination with towering figures of the Church such as Saint Joan of Arc, and her desire to imitate her French heroine. But one day God taught her a lasting lesson, one of the greatest graces she ever received. "He taught me that the only glory which matters is the glory which lasts forever, and that one does not have to perform shining deeds to win that." In fact, she believed that we should hide our acts of virtue even from ourselves. "Do not let your left hand know what your right hand is doing'" (Mt 6:3).

The Little Flower determined that she would win glory by becoming a saint, though her glory (in this life) would be hidden from the eyes of the world. She was all about trust and sacrifice, focusing her spiritual eyes on heaven and longing to be joined to Jesus. Thérèse didn't have to wait long — she died when she was twenty-four.

While Thérèse's earthly labor yielded immediate fruit, the real harvest took place in God's time. He's the great gardener in heaven; planting, watering, and pruning the little flowers in his garden like Thérèse. One of the great lessons we can learn from her life is that we must have patience and humility in the midst of our earthly labors, even when things don't look like they're going right. To earthly eyes, Jesus' death on the cross certainly didn't look like a victory, but it was. The long and the short of it is that evangelization takes time and will continue to the end of time.

Made for More

Though we find ourselves in a new era, the human person is still a human person. We're still doing the same dumb stuff we did from the beginning — it's not as if original sin has weakened over time. It's important, therefore, to recognize that the New Evangelization is new not in content but, as Pope Benedict has explained, in its "inner thrust." "'New' in ways that correspond with the power of the Holy Spirit and which are suited to the times and situations."[17]

In short, we still suffer from the same sickness, and so we still preach the same message as the apostles: Jesus Christ, who is "the same yesterday and today and for ever" (Heb 13:8). Even so, we seek a fresh outpouring of the Holy Spirit and fresh insights and opportunities that correspond to the needs of today.

We can do this with confidence because — at the risk of sounding over-the-top — Christianity holds the trump card. We've got the ace in the hole. The deck is stacked (and a bunch of other card idioms). Why? Because whether they know it or not, everybody is looking for what we have. We tend to shy away from evangelizing because what we're offering doesn't have the glitz and glamour of this world. It's easy to forget the power of what we possess.

On the other hand, there's no doubt that the initial conversation with a nonbeliever or someone struggling with faith can be daunting, if not terrifying. As far as I know, there is no book of evangelistic opening lines, but I strongly suggest that you avoid rolling up to someone and saying, "Didn't I see you at Easter Mass? Or was it Christmas?" Even worse would be, "Dude, want me to hook you up with a brown scapular?" Next time you meet, watch these people flee at your approach.

That being said, it isn't nearly as hard as you think. People are already looking, searching, digging for meaning in this life. The Rolling Stones made the desire for satisfaction one of the most famous rock lyrics ever. Everybody knows they can't get none, though they try, try, try. And this lack of satisfaction isn't only an issue for rock stars, it's the condition of all humans.

Recently, for example, I had a conversation with two of my children. We were cleaning their room, an activity often preceded by groans and protests, and as I pulled forgotten toys out of the dark recesses of their closet I playfully reminded them of how much they "had to have" or "really wanted" these toys when they were new. But as every parent knows, two weeks is the maximum life expectancy of a child's satisfaction with a new toy (unless it has no batteries, in which case life expectancy is reduced to seven and a half minutes).

Most post-pubescent people suffer from the same problem to one degree or another. No matter how much we have, we want more. And money, power, fame, the opposite sex, a big house and car — none of these things can satisfy. Yet we continue struggling for more, more, more. Why? Because we *were* made for more — more than this life has to offer.

At the end of the day, we can't get "enough" except through God. As Father Thomas Dubay used to say, "God is the divine Enough." This world is not our end, it is not our true home — and much of our angst stems from the fact that we act as if it is. God didn't make us so that we'd be born, get potty-trained, go to school, get a job, get married, have kids, retire, and die — if we're lucky enough to make it through all the stages. God created us, rather, for undreamed-of glory and unimaginable ecstasy in his presence. As Saint Paul said: "No eye has seen, nor ear heard, nor the heart of man conceived, what God has prepared for those who love him" (1 Cor 2:9).

We have something that no other created being has — a spiritual core with an intellect and a will. We can laugh. We can love. We can choose. We aren't simply driven by instinct like animals (with the exception of my Pavlovian response to oven-hot brownies).

In the final analysis, we are a union of body and spirit that can never be satisfied by this world because we were created to go beyond what we can see, taste, touch, and smell. We were created "by God and for God," the *Catechism* says (27), and only in the arms of our loving Father will we find what we're looking for.

Unfortunately, too many people are looking in all the wrong places. For example, Saint Augustine — bishop, theologian, and Doctor of the Church — is one of the most influential voices in the history of Christianity. He is cited more than any other writer in the *Catechism of the Catholic Church*, except for the authors of Scripture. Yet he lived a notoriously sinful life prior to his conversion, plunged early in life into a "whirlpool of shameful deeds."[18] It was years before he realized the vanity and emptiness of his ways. "I sought for you outside myself," he lamented in his famous *Confessions*, "but I did not find you, the God of my heart."

Like so many others, Augustine was searching for happiness. "Is not the happy life that which all men will to have?"[19] he asked. Yes! Everybody is searching. Everybody is seeking that elusive fulfillment. But he kept coming up empty because he was looking in all the wrong places. Everyone experiences this deep sense of dissatisfaction and lack of fulfillment at some point. Everybody's looking for answers even if they haven't yet put their finger on the question. Just as a person's hunger indicates the body's need for food, the very fact that we long for more points to the fact that there must be more than this unfulfilling life.[20]

Supply and Demand

In spite of the fact that we Catholics can help people with their search, we're not always sure how to get others to listen. Yet our joy in the Lord — evident in the way we live — will get people's attention. I'm not saying we should avoid learning to speak eloquently and knowledgeably about the Faith, but the fact that we've achieved even a modicum of peace and joy speaks volumes to a world that can only reproduce these in cheap imitation.

To his chagrin, Saint Augustine discovered peace in Christ only after he tried everything else. As he said in the opening pages of his *Confessions*, "You have made us for yourself, O Lord, and our hearts are restless until they rest in you."[21] This is what we offer the world; eternal rest in the Father.

When you think about it from a business perspective, Christians are sort of an economist's dream. Before a company decides to produce a product, it first analyzes the market to measure demand. No buyers, no product. But no such thing is necessary in our case. Our happiness and satisfaction actually create a market because the rest of the world wants what we have. Everyone we encounter has a built-in need for what we have to offer.

We must be prepared, however. We can't talk about, much less take up, a way of life that we don't understand. As Saint Basil warned, "without knowledge … we cannot be made like him, and knowledge cannot be achieved without lessons."[22] So let's do a little learning.

CHAPTER 4

LESSONS IN LOVE

IMAGINE YOU'RE IN THE MOST BEAUTIFUL, sweet smelling, awe-inspiring garden paradise ever. Incredible flowers of every color bloom all around you, bursting with a fragrance you can almost taste. A waterfall splashes and sparkles nearby. Off to your right, hanging on the greenest, most luscious tree you have ever seen, a juicy orange the size of a small satellite beckons your taste buds. To your left, a steaming cup of perfectly brewed espresso awaits the tender embrace of your fingers. (It wouldn't be paradise without it.) Everything is complete bliss in your garden paradise except for one tiny problem: someone is trying to kill you.

The Genesis of It All

Just as the message of Christ we want to live and share isn't new, neither is the evil we're battling. It all goes back to the beginning. In fact, what Jesus did for us on the cross is directly related to what happened in the Garden of Eden. "For as in Adam all die, so also in Christ shall all be made alive" (1 Cor 15:22). The Garden of Eden is directly tied to the Garden of Gethsemane.

Jesus didn't die only for our personal sins — that time you stole, that lie you told, that Sunday Mass you missed because you were wasting away in Margaritaville the night before. He died to deal with the root of the problem — the sin of Adam which affects all of us. Jesus came to restore life to a world that was dead through sin, because that was the result of Adam's sin — death. God had breathed into Adam's nostrils his *ruah* — his divine life — and this is what had made Adam immortal. But he lost his immortality when he sinned. And he lost the ability to pass it on to us.

When Adam and Eve disobeyed God and ate of the Tree of the Knowledge of Good and Evil, they committed the first mortal sin. They died spiritually and were cut off from their Maker, a fate far worse than the end of physical life (see CCC 399). Mankind was now dead through sin and needed to be brought back to life. God didn't lovingly make us in his image only to leave us once sin entered the picture — he always had a plan to restore us. That plan was his Son, Jesus Christ.

This isn't news for most of us, but perhaps we're a little too familiar with the story. Maybe we haven't peeled the onion back enough to appreciate fully what makes us cry out in joy every Easter. To understand our calling as Catholics and evangelizers of the world, we must understand exactly what it is that Christ did for us. Let's take a look.

In his letter to the Galatians, Saint Paul tells us that "when the time had fully come," God sent his Son Jesus to suffer and die for us so that we might "receive adoption as sons" (4:4-5). In other words, God wanted to restore us so we could rejoin his family. Adam wasn't just another creature in the garden; he was special; he was created to be a "son of God" (Lk 3:38). In fact, just like our first parents, we are all created to be children of God.

But as you know from the story, God took his sweet time before sending his Son after what took place in the Garden of Eden. Why? Partly because Adam had ably demonstrated the fact that mankind was nowhere near capable of living like a child of God — of giving himself back to God in the manner his Father wanted.

Instead, Adam chose himself over God. And that's something we need to unpack a bit, because it's the crux of the problem we face. In fact, really and truly understanding original sin changes everything. It's the key to unlocking what the Catholic faith is all about.

We don't know exactly what happened in the Garden. The *Catechism* says that "the account of the fall in *Genesis* 3 uses figurative language, but affirms a primeval event, a deed that took place *at the beginning of the history of man* ... (cf. *GS* 13, para. 1)" and that "the whole of human history is marked by the original fault freely committed by our first parents (cf. Council of Trent: DS 1513; Pius XII: DS 3897; Paul VI: AAS 58 [1966], 654)" (CCC 390).

We may not know exactly what Adam and Eve did, but it's pretty clear that somehow through pride, they rejected the idea of self-sacrifice, of self-gift, and gave in to the devil. We know this because Saint Paul tells us that Christ, the "Last Adam," came to do what the first

Adam did not (see 1 Cor 15:45). "For as by one man's disobedience many were made sinners, so by one man's obedience many will be made righteous" (Rom 5:19). The self-offering of Christ overcame the self-centered sin of Adam or, to put it yet another way, the sin of Adam and the subsequent action of Christ on the cross are the keys to understanding salvation — both what went wrong and how we are saved.

Making Sense of Sacrifice

Most of us have crucifixes around our houses, cars, and necks, but have you ever asked yourself why Jesus had to die on the cross? What is the logic behind it? Why didn't God just snap his fingers and put everything back in order? How do we make sense of Jesus' sacrifice? Understanding the nature of sacrifice and how sacrifice and humanity are related will help us begin to answer these questions.

Pope Benedict XVI has pointed out that "in all religions, sacrifice is at the heart of worship."[23] The reason is simple: exterior sacrifice symbolizes interior sacrifice. Anyone familiar with history knows that sacrifice isn't associated only with Christianity. Many faiths have practiced sacrifice, some quite extreme. Aztec Indians, for example, sacrificed up to twenty thousand people a year by tearing out their hearts and hurling their bodies down from temple pyramids. They did this to appease their sun god. Rejecting FDA recommendations to the contrary, they actually ate the flesh of their victims. And the Old

Testament books of Leviticus and Second Kings refer to a horrifying religion in which children were offered as sacrificial victims to the pagan god Molech (see Lv 18:21; 20:2-5; 2 Kgs 23:10).

Of course there are other, shall we say, less historical examples of the ingrained need for sacrifice in human religious expression. *King Kong* and *Indiana Jones and the Temple of Doom*, for instance. Even the king's daughter that Saint George rescued from the dragon was being offered up in sacrifice.

Whether real or fabled, these and other examples underscore the fact that sacrifice has been part of religious practice throughout human history. It's written into our DNA. Of course, I'm betting that you want to know why.

Like Totally

The first chapter of Genesis tells us that we were originally made in the "image and likeness" of God (Gn 1:26-27). We can't begin to grasp what that means until we try to wrap our puny minds around the "central mystery of the Christian faith and of Christian life," the Trinity (CCC 261). Of course, we can't actually plumb the depths of the infinite God. As Blessed Columba Marmion put it, we can only "stammer" when talking about the Trinity.[24] Th-th-th-that being said, there are at least some things we know.

For starters, we know that God has revealed himself as our Father, and Jesus is his Son. And we also know how they relate to one another, in total self-gift.[25] The Father totally gives himself to the Son, and the Son gives of himself totally back to the Father. And from this mutual self-donation, this mutual love, eternally proceeds the Third Person, the Holy Spirit.

Does that sound familiar? It should, because our families are a reflection of the Holy Trinity — they are icons, images of God. The members of our families may not be eternal, coequal beings like God, but our relationships still mimic those of the Trinity. In a loving marriage, the husband gives himself totally to his wife. His wife, in return, gives herself completely to her husband. And what proceeds from this love communion? A third person that is so important that you spend nine months vainly attempting to come up with the perfect name.

So the Trinity is a community of divine persons who constantly make a complete offering of themselves to each other. To put it differently, the Father, Son, and Holy Spirit form a sacrificial family. And we were made to be a part of this family. So God created Adam and Eve in his "image and likeness."

But when Adam sinned in the Garden, he (and the rest of us, doggone it!) lost the likeness to God, though we are still made in his image (see CCC 2566). This is what the Christian life is all about — reclaiming the likeness to God that was lost in the Garden.

Give Until It Hurts

Of course, this leaves us with a huge question. How do

we define this likeness? What is it that God does that we're called to do? Exactly this: loving self-donation, self-sacrifice, total self-gift. These are the things that make us like God because loving, sacrificial self-giving is what he does. As the Second Vatican Council stated: man "cannot fully find himself except through a sincere gift of himself."[26]

To help us get back our likeness to him, God instituted a system of sacrifice that is designed to teach us how to sacrifice *ourselves* — how to be like him. In reading the Old Testament you've probably come across stories featuring the slaughter of animals. It wasn't pretty, and for a long period of Israelite history it happened every day. If you were a bull, sheep, or goat in Old Testament Israel, there was no point in contributing to a retirement plan. You'd never live to see it.

While it might disturb our modern sensibilities, animal sacrifice played a central role in the life of the Israelites. These sacrifices weren't for God's sake, however. He's never been some divine egomaniac demanding that we give him homage. Nor did he ever have some vendetta against cute farm animals. Rather, the sacrifices he required were for our sake. He demanded the first fruits of the harvest and the best animals as offerings because it taught us to give the best we have back to him. And, ultimately, the best we can offer is ourselves.

You'd be hard pressed to find someone who offered himself up quite like Saint Lawrence, the patron saint of gridirons (and I ain't talkin' football). Lawrence was a third-century deacon in Rome during the persecutions of Valerian. Arrested after he refused to turn over the wealth of the Church to Roman authorities, he was sentenced to death by roasting (hence his patronage of gridirons, chefs, and cooks).

In spite of his gruesome death, Saint Lawrence is perhaps most remembered for his black(ened) humor. The story goes that joking with his executioners while being burned alive, he proffered some cooking advice: "Turn me over," he said. "I'm done on this side."

Love Is the Key

What is it that makes a saint like Lawrence give himself up so easily, cracking jokes as he's dying? Quite simply, love. Lawrence and countless saints throughout history have loved God so much they were willing to die for him. That's true love.

Now perhaps you're thinking, "Fire-roasted is all well and good for things like nuts and marshmallows, but it doesn't fit my idea of love. To be honest, that sounds more like suffering." Fair enough. I think you're on to something. So let's dig a little deeper and talk about love, a word we toss around fairly casually in our contemporary culture.

We're familiar with the sight of a smitten couple professing their love to each other in soft whispers. But it's not unusual to hear a guy say to his buddy, "I love you, man" after they've shared some deep, brotherly moment (usually involving sports). Or to hear a woman exclaim how much she just loves her new shoes while surrounded by a gaggle of other ladies ogling her feet. We have only one word for love in English, but depending on the context it means different things.

The ancient Greeks, on the other hand, had several words for the various meanings of love. *Eros* meant erotic or romantic love, *philia* was the love found in friendship, and *agape* (or *caritas* in Latin) is the word for self-giving love.

These words reflect different types of love, but we're interested in something more. We want to know what love is in its essence. The most obvious place to look for that definition is sacred Scripture, the Word of God. Scripture tells us, of course, that "God is love" (1 Jn 4:8). He doesn't have love. He *is* love. It drives who he is and what he does. And what did he do? According to the Gospel of John, "God so loved the world that he gave his only son, that whoever believes in him should not perish but have eternal life" (3:16).

So love has to do with giving. More to the point, as we discussed earlier, it has to do with *self*-giving. As Pope Benedict XVI notes in his encyclical *Deus Caritas Est* (*"God Is Love"*), "love is ... a journey ... an ongoing exodus out of the closed inward-looking self towards its liberation through self-giving ... and thus towards the discovery of God" (6).

Unfortunately, humanity in general tends to be pretty self-centered, and so the love we focus on and elevate is *eros*, romantic love. And in the hands of a fallen world, *eros* easily turns into vice.

I'm not old enough to remember the 1960s, but many think of that era of long hair and so-called free love as the perfect example of *eros* gone wrong. (For them, Woodstock doesn't equal Snoopy.) But *eros* gone wrong started a long time before hippies and bell-bottoms.

As Pope Benedict notes in his encyclical, in pre-Christian times the elevation and distortion of *eros* led to fertility cults and temple prostitution (4). The ancients knew that there was a relationship between love and the divine, but like the long-haired, freaky people of the 1960s, they elevated and distorted *eros*. They submitted the divine to mere instinct, seeking to achieve communion with their pagan gods through erotic ecstasy.

In light of this history, it's interesting to note that the Old Testament uses the word *eros* only twice and the New Testament doesn't use it at all. Why? Because, says Pope Benedict, there is "something new and distinct about the Christian understanding of love" (3).

Now don't get me wrong. Even though a lot of people accuse Christians of being prudes, Christianity doesn't shy away from *eros*; it celebrates it. We recognize that *eros* is what makes the soul grow wings and soar upward toward divine beauty. It reflects the longing for beauty that lives in every person's heart.

Indeed, Scripture often describes the relationship between God and his people in romantic, marital terms. You see this erotic language in books such as Hosea, Ezekiel, and the sometimes PG-13-rated Song of Songs: "You are all fair, my love; there is no flaw in you. Come with me from Lebanon, my bride ... How sweet is your love, my sister, my bride! How much better is your love than wine, and the fragrance of your oils than any spice!" (4:7-8,10). (Slap that on a Valentine's Day card, gentlemen.)

Be that as it may, *eros* is only one side of the coin. Christian love must also include agape love — sacrificial self-gift directed toward the other, the kind of love that wants the best for the beloved. This is the love of God.

The Almost Sacrifice of Isaac

It shouldn't surprise us, then, that the very first time the word *love* is used in the Bible is in the context of one of the greatest stories ever told of self-offering, that of Abraham and Isaac. The Book of Genesis recounts that God asked Abraham to do the unthinkable: sacrifice the son whom he had waited for his whole life, the son he never thought he would have. "Take your son, your only son Isaac, whom you love, and go to the land of Mori'ah, and offer him there as a burnt offering upon one of the mountains of which I shall tell you" (Gn 22:2)

And I can relate to Abraham. I've been blessed with three girls and one boy (so far), and I wouldn't trade my girls for the world. But after my first two offspring were of the female persuasion, I was ready for some testosterone to even things out. It took five long years of ballet lessons, Barbie dolls, and the wrong kind of nail parties before my wish for a son was granted. Of course, my plight was nothing like that of Abraham. God asked old Abe to take the boy for which he had waited one hundred years and offer him up as a sacrifice on Moriah.

So here's what we have: a father giving up his beloved only son, and a son who not only accompanies his dad, but carries the wood for the sacrifice up the mountain. The son, whom scholars point out is not a toddler but likely a young man, actually allows himself to be bound by his father and is ready to offer himself in sacrifice.[27] Having grown up in a world where sacrifice was not uncommon, Isaac knows what's going down. Talk about obedience!

So the father gives up his only son, and the son gives himself up to the wishes of the father. Each of them is willing to make what he considers to be the ultimate sacrifice. My guess is that you already see where this is going. Scholars throughout the ages have recognized the "almost" sacrifice of Isaac to be a foreshadowing of the sacrifice of Jesus on the cross. He's the beloved only Son of the Father who carries the wood for his own sacrifice up the mountain and offers himself.

Of course, God the Father and Jesus the Son actually did what wasn't required of Abraham to complete. And in so doing, they revealed to us the essence of love. "I give you a new commandment: love one another. As I have loved you, so you also should love one another" (Jn 13:34, NAB) And what does this love look like? Jesus himself tells us: "No one has greater love than this, to lay down one's life for one's friends" (Jn 15:13, NAB). It's all about death to self for the sake of the other. "Greater love" is life-giving love.

To the Max

Perhaps no modern saint exemplifies "greater love" better than Saint Maximilian Kolbe. Dubbed by Blessed John Paul II as "the patron saint of our difficult century," Kolbe was a Polish priest prior to and during the difficult years of World War II. When Kolbe was a child, he had a vision of the Blessed Virgin Mary. In the vision, Our Lady offered him the choice between two crowns, one white and one red — the white stood for a life of purity, the red for martyrdom. Kolbe chose both.

While his life as a priest gave him ample opportunity to practice purity, World War II provided his coronation as a martyr. The Nazis discovered that Kolbe was harboring Jews in his friary and arrested him. In the spring of 1941, Kolbe — prisoner number 16670 — was processed into the Auschwitz concentration camp. In July of the same year, three prisoners escaped from the camp, provoking the commandant, in retribution, to send ten men into an underground bunker to be starved to death. Upon being chosen, one of the men cried out in agony, "What will happen to my family?" Hearing this, Kolbe stepped calmly out of line and offered himself as a substitute.[28] Surprisingly, the commandant agreed.

Once in the bunker, Kolbe led the other men in constant song and prayer as, one by one, they died. After two weeks, the four men who remained alive were injected with carbolic acid to hasten the inevitable and clear the cell for other prisoners. It is said that Fr. Kolbe raised his arm to receive the lethal dose from his executioner. His coronation complete, his captors cremated his remains on the feast of the Assumption.

I first heard of Saint Maximilian Kolbe around the time I was received into the Church. His story made me wonder about myself. Did I possess that same strength? Would I be willing to do the same thing? I wanted to believe that I would, but I wasn't sure.

Sometimes when we read the lives of saints like Kolbe, we view them like black-and-white reruns in our mind's eye, a story from so long ago it's almost otherworldly. But we face many of the same challenges the saints did, though our challenges may manifest themselves in different ways.

When you get down to it, every day in the life of a Christian is preparation for death. It may not be the most pleasant thought, but there's no way around it. Because of Adam's fall, "death spread to all men," says Saint Paul (Rom 5:12). In other words, nobody's gettin' out of here alive.

CHAPTER 5

BEER, CHOCOLATE, AND VALUE-ADDED SUFFERING

WHILE STUDYING IN EUROPE shortly after my conversion to Catholicism, I had the opportunity to visit Rome. One of my most lasting memories is of the Bone Church.

Otherwise known as Santa Maria della Concezione dei Cappuccini, the Bone Church garners its name from its basement crypt that harbors the remains of more than four thousand Capuchin friars. Well-known authors and others have visited and commented on it, people such as Mark Twain, Nathaniel Hawthorne, and the Marquis de Sade, who wrote, "I have never seen anything more striking."[29] (Quite a statement, coming from that guy.)

What's so striking about the Bone Church? The rounded walls and ceiling of the dimly lit crypt are literally covered with human bones, many of them in terrifying shapes. (I'll never forget looking up to see a bony Grim Reaper hovering over me.) The place is spooky, to say the least — so much so that the professor who brought me there waited outside while I went in alone.

From start to finish, time spent in the crypt is focused on death. And it's not just other people's demise you're thinking about as you silently make your way through the dimly lit alcoves. The friars make sure the intended message is loud, clear, and personal. Near one of the hewn-out little alcove chapels hangs a plaque that reads: "What you are now, we once were; what we are now, you shall be."

The point made in so startling a manner by the Bone Church is that the "art of living" isn't just about evangelization; it's about preparation for the end of our lives. Like so many other saints and martyrs, Saint Maximilian Kolbe, whom we met in the last chapter, had been pouring out his life for years. His death at the hands of the Nazis was only the final blow. Picking up his cross on a daily basis, Kolbe dedicated himself to imitating Christ so that when the time came he was fully prepared to offer himself in the place of another. It had become the natural thing to do. A Protestant doctor who treated patients in Kolbe's prison block attested to this: "From my observations ... the virtues in the Servant of God were no momentary impulse such as were often found in men; they sprang from a habitual practice, deeply woven into his personality."[30]

The ability to be like Christ, to offer oneself up for another, typically involves a lifetime of growth that starts in the little things, such as learning how to turn our daily sufferings into something good. Believe it or not, this is one of the coolest things about being Catholic — suffering.

Before you put down this book and walk away convinced I'm a lunatic, think about it. I don't mean that we suffer more because we're Catholic, or that we masochistically enjoy it. I mean that the Church's view of human suffering brings more blessing to the table than any "health and wealth" doctrine I've ever encountered. If you're still scratching your head, allow me to break it down.

Designed to Discipline

The question of suffering has occupied humanity since the Fall. We can't escape suffering. Where did it come from? What is its meaning? If God really loves us, why do we suffer? The fact of suffering has even caused many people to lose their faith, to give up hope. But because we are saved by the cross of Christ, a new value has been given to this inevitable fact of human existence. A brief survey of Scripture will show us various approaches to suffering over time — and reveal some of the reasons I think it's one of the best things about being Catholic.

Beginning in the Old Testament, we see that suffering was most often viewed as the result of sin. If you were suffering, you must have done something wrong. It was punishment, plain and simple.

But in the story of Job, we learn that not all suffering is the direct result of wickedness. Job was a very holy guy who offered sacrifices every day for his children just in case they did something wrong. What a great dad! Scripture makes it clear that he suffered even though he was innocent. Who does that remind you of? (Hint: His name starts with a "J" and rhymes with "esus.")

In fact, we learn that Job suffered because his righteousness was being tested. Satan didn't think Job would remain true to God if he endured hardship. God therefore allowed him to suffer in order to prove Job's faithfulness, demonstrating that suffering can happen to people no matter how good they are.

On the other hand, we learn from various stories of the Israelites that sometimes there is indeed a connection between suffering and sin. The Israelites often endured hardship because of the sins they committed out of their "hardness of heart" (Mt 19:8).

But their punishments weren't simply punishments, per se. They were "designed not to destroy but to discipline" the Israelites (2 Mc 6:12). Why? Because Israel was God's "first-born son," which means God was the Israelites' Father (Ex 4:22) bringing his children to maturity and teaching them how to live rightly. Indeed, as the Letter to the Hebrews tells us, "the Lord disciplines him whom he loves" (12:6).

Still, it is not until the divine love of the cross that we begin to grasp the "why" of suffering. In the new covenant of Christ, the true nature of suffering is revealed.

When Jesus offered himself back to the Father on the cross for our sake, he didn't merely deal with the consequences of sin. Rather, he was striking at the root of suffering — original sin, the sin of Adam (see Rom 5:15). And when Christ, the "Last Adam," conquered death, dealing with sin at its source, he did it in a way that seems crazy in the eyes of the world (see 1 Cor 15:45). He took the consequences of sin (suffering and death), experienced them as one of us, and made them the path to salvation.

Think about that. Jesus became a man specifically to suffer and die, to experience the full weight of human sin. And since our salvation comes through being "imitators of God," we are to follow in Christ's footsteps, becoming "a fragrant offering and sacrifice to God" (Eph 5:1-2). If you want to rise like Christ, you have to suffer and die like Christ. "United with him in a death like his," says Paul, "we shall certainly be united with him in a resurrection like his" (Rom 6:5).

And so in Christ we find the key that unlocks everything: the secret ingredient of redemptive suffering isn't misery; it's love. Pain doesn't overcome death. If they had driven fewer nails into Christ's body or whipped him a little less, we still would have been saved. The pain he experienced was awful, but that's not what saved us. Rather, the Father gave us the Son out of love (Jn 3:16), and the Son gives himself back to us and the Father out of love. "Love is strong as death," the Song of Songs tells us (8:6). "Love covers a multitude of sins" echoes the First Letter of Peter (4:8).

In fact, Blessed John Paul II said that "suffering is present in the world in order to release love, in order to give birth to works of love towards neighbor, in order to transform the whole of human civilization into a 'civilization of love.' "[31] Suffering and death are tied to love through Christ. We discover our humanity, dignity, vocation, and mission through suffering united to the cross of Jesus.

Christ shows us our calling. Driven by love, we are to pick up our crosses and sufferings and follow Our Lord. This is the way to resurrection and life (see Mt 16:24). Indeed, suffering is the face of love. This is true charity. This is the path to sanctity and life eternal. Even when suffering is the consequence of our sinful actions, it is an opportunity for growth.

Value-Added Suffering

Perhaps right now you're looking for an exit, an escape hatch: "Dang, Matt! Am I supposed to go around seeking out suffering?" Well, let's be honest. You and I both know it's going to happen, one way or another. You can run, but you can't hide. I don't care if you have all the money in the world; you can't buy suffering insurance. There's no getting around the fact that in this fallen world, we're going to suffer. Instead of despairing, we should be thankful that suffering has been given eternal value by Christ.

Further, our suffering is either going to take place now or it's going to take place later. The cross might have dealt with the eternal consequences of our sin, but there are still temporal consequences. The piper is going to get paid. Even if we are destined for heaven, we're going to feel it in purgatory if we don't suffer first on earth.

That being said, the difference between earthly suffering and the suffering we undergo in purgatory (assuming we make it) is huge. There's a big bonus associated with earthly suffering: Whether it's the result of penances or just happens to us, earthly suffering can be voluntarily joined to the suffering of Christ and become redemptive.

In other words, if we make an act of the will and offer up our sufferings to the Lord, that act becomes powerful, not just for ourselves but for others. That's why Saint Paul can say, "I rejoice in my sufferings for your sake, and in my flesh I complete what is lacking in Christ's afflictions for the sake of his body, that is, the church" (Col 1:24).

But let's be clear. Jesus' perfect offering doesn't *need* our participation — his sacrifice was completely sufficient for our redemption. But he wills that we participate in his sufferings because this is the path of salvation. It's how we regain our likeness to him.

The passion, death, and resurrection of Jesus endows human suffering with redemptive value that it would never have on its own. On its own, suffering is just that — suffering. But now we can "rejoice in our sufferings" because *his* suffering gives it eternal value (Rom 5:3). This is so because "it is no longer I who live, but Christ who lives in me" (Gal 2:20). At our baptism we were incorporated into the Mystical Body of Christ and, now, everything we experience, all of our joys and sufferings, are joined to him through whom "we live and move and have our being" (Acts 17:28).

Buried Alive

We tend to associate baptism with beautiful little babies, however, not with suffering. And it's true that there are few things better than the sweet smell of chrism oil and the sight of relatives packed around the baptismal font, holding their breath to see if the baby will wail when the water streams across his or her forehead. (It's practically dogma in the minds of some that if a baby boy doesn't cry, he's going to be a priest.)

Indeed, baptisms are beautiful. I like to do what Saint Francis did whenever he witnessed a child's new birth in Christ. He genuflected because this infant now possessed the full indwelling of the Holy Trinity. Thrice immersed, the baby had become a living tabernacle.

Baptism is ultimately about new life, but we should not neglect its full significance. On one hand, it replaces the sanctifying grace lost by Adam in the Garden, and so we are "freed from sin and reborn as sons of God" (CCC 1213). It's the sacrament that opens the door to the rest of the sacraments.

On the other hand, the *Catechism* tells us that baptism symbolizes our "burial into Christ's death," from which we are resurrected with him as "'a new creature' (2 *Cor* 5:17; *Gal* 6:15; cf. *Rom* 6:3-4; *Col* 2:12)" (CCC 1214). Baptism by immersion — when the whole person is briefly dunked under water three times — vividly symbolizes this death and resurrection. Far more than an occasion for a family get-together, baptism is a statement about how the life of the baptized is going to play out. Before the first candidate ever descended into the water, Jesus himself made this clear in his encounter with the mother of the apostles James and John.

The Gospel of Mark recalls that the mother of these apostles rolled up to Jesus, boys in tow, wanting to make sure they were taken care of in this new kingdom Jesus kept talking about. Jesus was assuredly aware of her intention, but do you remember his response to her request to have her boys sit at his right and left hand in heaven? He said, "You do not know what you are asking. Are you able to drink the cup that I drink, or to be baptized with the baptism with which I am baptized?" (Mk 10:38).

They probably said something along the lines of "No problem, Jesus!" They didn't think it was any big deal because they didn't understand exactly what Jesus was talking about. And you can't blame James and John's mom for trying to help out her boys. It's what any good mother does — try to take care of her family. What she (and her boys) didn't yet grasp is what it means to be on the right and left of Christ. But she found out. The next time she appears is at the foot of the cross, gazing upon the two thieves hanging on either side of Our Lord. I can only imagine what she was thinking of her request then.

And so it is that the baptized, joined to the mystical body of Christ, now find that all their actions have an impact on the rest of the members of the Mystical Body. Suffering — both involuntary suffering and voluntary penances — offered up to God can become a path to holiness for the one who suffers, and grace for the rest of the body of Christ. This isn't optional. Saint Paul makes it clear it is the path to heaven: "We are ... fellow heirs with Christ, provided we suffer with him in order that we may also be glorified with him" (Rom 8:17).

Beer and Chocolate

Right about now you might be saying to yourself: "Sheesh, Matt, you make it sound so great — suffer this and offer up that. Who would want to be part of this family? Is this the unimaginable ecstasy you were talking about before?" Kind of!

Consider the last part of that verse from Romans: If we suffer with him we'll be *glorified* with him. In the next verse Paul says "that the sufferings of this present time are not worth comparing with the glory that is to be revealed to us" (8:18). Remember, you're going to suffer anyway because of sin. But if you embrace it and offer it up with Christ, it leads to new life.

We're all aware of involuntary suffering, but let's focus for a moment on voluntary penance, because it's a bit of a different animal. We do it every Advent and Lent, and perhaps at other times. Why do women give up chocolate and men give up beer? It's not that these are bad things. God created the whole world and declared it "very good" (Gn 1:31). There's nothing wrong with chocolate or beer. Some of my best friends are chocolate and beer!

The role voluntary penance serves is this: it takes our eyes off ourselves. It's not about the chocolate or the beer, in and of themselves. Yes, we need to challenge ourselves by giving up something that we enjoy or is important to us — doing so reveals our love for and willingness to suffer for Jesus. But at its root, voluntary penance is about giving ourselves. It's about making an offering of ourselves to God and to our neighbor.

Voluntary penance demonstrates the distinct relationship between love and sacrifice. Wasn't that why the song "Love Hurts" was written? Perhaps I'm wrong, but the fact that the name of the band who recorded it is Nazareth must lend at least *some* credence to my argument. But if 1970s pop music isn't the authority you're looking for, allow me to refer you to Saint Thérèse of Lisieux. She said that "true love feeds on sacrifice, and becomes more pure and strong the more our natural satisfaction is denied."[32]

That's a pretty powerful statement. Too bad Solomon couldn't have caught the petals of wisdom that fell from the Little Flower. He could have used them.

The Dumbest Wise Man Ever

Most of us are familiar with the story of King Solomon. And most of us tend to view him in a positive light because of his great wealth and smarts. But to me, Solomon's story is one of the scariest in the Bible because he's a perfect example of how uncontrolled passion can destroy a person. (Not to mention that Solomon's my middle name.)

Solomon was without a doubt the most popular kid on the block. His pop, King David, was the great warrior king of Israel, a man after God's own heart. Not only was he David's boy, but even God himself said Solomon shall be "my son" (2 Sm 7:14). (When your natural father is known for killing lions, bears, and giants, and your supernatural Father is the Creator of the universe, nobody in your elementary school ever threatens that his dad could beat up your dad.)

After David passed his throne to his son, the Lord spoke to King Solomon and said, "Ask what I shall give you" (1 Kgs 3:5-9). Solomon asked for wisdom so that he could rule justly, a request that pleased God so much that he gave him wisdom in spades, as well as great wealth and long life. Even more special, God gave him the privilege of building the Temple in Jerusalem, God's permanent dwelling place on earth. And during Solomon's reign, people from all over the world came to worship in God's house and hear the wisdom of the great king. Solomon's reign was the high point of the kingdom of Israel. Put simply, he had it going on.

But even with all those God-given smarts, Solomon made massive mistakes. Way back in Deuteronomy, right before the Israelites were going to enter into the Promised Land of Israel, Moses had given some instructions and warnings. He told the Israelites that when they had a king (which wouldn't happen for another five hundred years or so), he was not to multiply three things: weapons, wealth, or wives. Solomon didn't follow Moses' instructions. In fact, he did everything he wasn't supposed to do. Though God had blessed him with a lot of cold cash, the sinister sin of greed took root. Solomon imposed heavy taxes upon the Israelites in his desire for more wealth. He also greatly over-built his army and navy.

But perhaps the most shocking thing this "wise" man did was marry seven hundred times. (No wonder the taxes were so high. Can you imagine the credit-card bills?) Not only that, he added three hundred concubines to his harem.

To add insult to injury, many of the women he "married" didn't know or worship the true God, and Solomon allowed them to build altars to their false gods and to worship them. Ultimately, this led to his own departure from the faith and the downfall of the entire kingdom.

How could a guy like Solomon lose his way so badly? He was the cat's meow, the sharpest knife in the drawer, the top of the heap — and he fell flat on his face. Do I, a guy whose elevator will never go as high as Solomon's, even stand a chance? How can I keep from making the same sorts of mistakes?

Appetite for Destruction

Part of the answer can be found in the writings of Saint John of the Cross, the sixteenth-century Spanish mystic and Doctor of the Church who achieved a very intimate relationship with Our Lord. Solomon might have been the wisest, but this cat was one of the holiest. And therein lies the rub: smarts don't equal salvation. (Thank goodness!) Unlike John, Solomon forgot who had given him his gifts and focused on created things instead of on his Creator. Saint John points out that Solomon's biggest mistake was that he couldn't control his passions.[33]

Perhaps you're thinking, "No joke, Matt! The dude had seven hundred wives!" But Solomon's carnal desires were only a symptom of what John is talking about. What led Solomon to abandon God in his old age was the fact that his intellect had been darkened and his will had become weak. Separated from God he could no longer see clearly. His desire to satisfy his lust and please his idolatrous wives gradually cost him his wisdom. Essentially, Saint John identifies Solomon's inability to control all of his appetites and impulses as the reason for his demise.

This is where the penance we've been talking about becomes so important. We must reign in all of our appetites and disordered desire for pleasure, not allowing them to control us.

Don't get me wrong. We're meant to enjoy this world. I'm not saying otherwise. This world is wonderful, and as Saint James says, "every perfect gift is from above" (Jas 1:17). Even so, our earthly existence isn't the end. We are striving for something infinitely better and more beautiful, which means we must develop a healthy detachment from this "lower" world regardless of how good it is.

Of course, detaching ourselves from the goods of this world isn't easy, and worse yet, John tells us that to do so we have to go beyond mortification and penance. They deal only with the result, not the cause of our disordered appetites. To deal with the cause, we need to pour weed-killer on the root of the bad appetite, burning out the actual desire for things that lead us away from God. That's a tall order.

We can do it, however, through the grace of God and our own determined efforts. Our job is to get rid of anything and everything that would cause us to stray from God. We're talking about more than just giving up beer and chocolate for Lent. This is about making a decision that we won't allow anything in our lives that isn't of Christ, and then continually acting on that decision. If that television show is nothing but trash, stop watching. In fact, throw out the TV if you need to. If that music is full of unholy garbage, stop listening. If that Dairy Queen tempts you to gluttony every time you drive by, find another route. (Or at least order a smaller Blizzard.)

Freedom to Give

The goal is to conform our will to Christ's. Penance quells our fleshly desires, preventing them from mastering us. It keeps us from being slaves to our bodily passions and frees us so that we are in control, so that we have possession of ourselves. This self-possession, this freedom, is critical. As Blessed John Paul II taught, you have to possess yourself before you can give yourself away.[34] You can't give what you don't own. If you're ruled by your passions, then you aren't free to give of yourself completely. That's why penance is so powerful. It's all about freedom and self-gift. The chocolate and the beer are means to an end, and the end is self-donation, not an opportunity to lose a little weight.

Ultimately, when we practice penance, we are giving up something good for something better. We're sacrificing the temporal goods of this world for the eternal "greats" of the next. We're voluntarily taming our own wants and desires in order to free our eyes to look to heaven and humbly identify with the actions of Our Lord. That's the power of penance. It detaches us from the things of this world so that we can act out of heavenly love.

At the end of the day, we need to move away from the idea that suffering is to be avoided at all costs, and view it instead in terms of sacrificial love. The cross has made it so. It was an act of love which calls us to the same. "If any man would come after me," Jesus said, "let him deny himself and take up his cross daily and follow me." We do so because "whoever loses his life for my sake, he will save it" (Lk 9:23-24).

Essentially, Jesus is telling us to do what he did. Give yourself away. That's what the golden rule is all about. We love God and our neighbor by giving ourselves to them completely.

Living in Love

But let's be honest. Sometimes it can be hard to love the people around us. Other people can be so annoying (though I'm sure I never am). There are assuredly those who get under your skin, people you've tried to get along with, but it's just not happening. It's a fact of life.

One way to tackle this is to offer up some penance for those who cause you suffering. If you just laughed out loud or your stomach involuntarily tightened, I don't blame you. My natural inclination is to make my "enemies" suffer, not suffer for them — but I hope you're much holier than I am. What I try to do to overcome my unholy aspirations is to imagine how Christ sees this person. I consider that one day, this person and I may be in heaven together. The same destiny I hope for — union with God for eternity — is the destiny of this person as well.

Of course, it's not as if Jesus thinks it's easy for us to love others. This is one of the reasons he tells us to love others as much as we love ourselves (see Mt 22:36-40). There's no getting around the fact that we have a tendency to look out for No. 1. If there's a mirror around, we're looking at ourselves. Front seat of the car? Mine! Pictures of other people? Boring! Our primary love and concern is for ourselves. Knowing this, Jesus calls us to extend that same love to others.

It can be done. The secret to loving other people is to love Christ. Only through him do we receive the graces to live and love as we're supposed to. We can't do it on our own — we're still fighting against inclinations that have plagued humanity since the Garden of Eden. But when Christ came and restored us to life, he gave us his Holy Spirit so that we could live and love as the Trinity does, in self-donation.

We're not just conjuring up emotion here: we're doing the right thing; we're practicing Spirit-driven virtue on a daily basis. As we do, we become more like the Lord, the veil of sin lifts, and we love him more. Growing close to Christ, beginning to act like him, is how we receive the grace to love others as he does.

Francis and the Leper

The story of Saint Francis and the leper drives this message home. Francis was something of a playboy in his "pre"-saint days. Born into wealth, he partied with the beautiful people and enjoyed the finer things of the world. In fact, he reveled in them.

Gladly answering the call to fight during the era of the Crusades, Francis had an elegant suit of armor made and was prepared to ride off to war, declaring, "I shall come back a great prince."[35] (Lack of confidence was not one of his issues.) Glory was his goal, and he was going to look good attaining it.

God had other plans. The night before he left, Francis had a vision of shields, swords, and armor all bearing the sign of the cross. To our intrepid wannabe knight, it seemed to be confirmation that his thirst for glory was about to be quenched.

But not long after departing the city limits of Assisi, Francis experienced a relapse of a sickness that had recently plagued him. On top of that, he had another dream in which God told him he had misinterpreted his previous vision. (I hate it when that happens.) In the second dream he was told to go back to town. Disappointed, humiliated, and sick as a dog, he returned to Assisi. It was during this time of somewhat depressed and listless wandering about the countryside that he had an experience of what it means to love others as Christ does. It proved to be a turning point.

One day he was on horseback outside the city when he saw a leper. Paralyzed by fear, he halted. This disgustingly disfigured man was the epitome of the ugliness that had always repulsed the little Italian. But then something amazing happened. Filled by what can only be described as grace, he vaulted from his horse, rushed to the stricken man, and threw his arms around him. And he didn't just provide emotional comfort, he gave the man cold, hard cash to help with his physical needs.

With a sense of peace and joy, Francis rode off from the encounter. As the story goes, when he turned around the leper was gone. Was it an angel? Was it Christ himself? We don't know. What we do know is that Francis had turned a corner. Having overcome his deep-seated, natural aversion to the sick and diseased, he had begun to love like Christ. What followed is a legendary life of loving service to the poor and the afflicted.

Let's Not Be Frank

What Francis and many others have figured out is that life is not about our own glory, we're not supposed to do it "my way," as Frank Sinatra used to sing. Jesus was very clear about this: "Whoever seeks to gain his life will lose it, but whoever loses his life will preserve it" (Lk 17:33).

Christ came to make this possible. It's no cakewalk, but the benefits are literally out of this world.

CHAPTER 6

HEAVEN: WHAT IT'S ALL ABOUT

As CATHOLICS WE HEAR A GREAT DEAL about this fallen world and how it affects us. This is appropriate because we have to know where we are before we can figure out where we're going. But let's turn our attention now in another direction — up. That's what all this self-donation and striving is aiming for: heaven.

We have to acknowledge upfront that we don't know exactly what heaven is. After all, Saint Paul said that "no eye has seen, nor ear heard, nor the heart of man conceived, what God has prepared for those who love him" (1 Cor 2:9). Even so, heaven is the destination. It's the goal! It's the prize! Why are we working out our salvation "with fear and trembling" (Phil 2:12)? Why are we offering up our sufferings? Why are we trying to control our worldly inclinations and to be like Christ? Because of heaven!

We need some motivation to stay the course, however, so let's provide some for ourselves by considering the heavenly reward for all this work. It'll be like when you were in a contest in school. Remember how they would always spur you on by showing you the prize before you competed?

Chicken Run

We lived in a rural area of Illinois when I was in first grade. Every year there was a county fair with rides and farm animals, snow cones and cotton candy — pure Americana. I loved the games best, especially the contest that pitted a chicken against a pack of highly motivated first graders. "Highly motivated" because the prize for being the first to catch the chicken was a silver dollar. To a first grader, a silver dollar was a fortune. I wanted it bad — real bad. Having spent a fair bit of my early years fleeing older brothers and their evil designs, I was well equipped to track down a flightless bird that sported legs even shorter than mine. Nobody else stood a chance. That chicken was mine.

In the winner's circle (a patch of dirt) I received an unexpected bonus. Not only did I win the silver, but the chicken, too. Finally, a pet to call my own. My parents were a bit reluctant to welcome the new member of our family because we lived in town and didn't really have a place for the chicken to live. But I begged, and so my chicken moved into the basement stairwell. We didn't have a dog, so I looked forward to coming home from school and hanging out with my chicken. (Yes, this came up in counseling.) But, alas, it was loud, and it stank. After a week, my parents had had enough. They gave it to a local farmer.

That saddened me, but not nearly as much as discovering twenty years later that we actually ate that chicken for Sunday dinner not long after it went to "live" at the farmer's house.

Perhaps small coins and poultry don't exactly set you on fire, but they sure looked good to a little boy. The point is that I saw the prize and would not be denied.

What Can We Know about Heaven?

I would be willing to bet that most of us have spent more time thinking about hell than heaven. It's a little easier to picture. Growing up as a Protestant I attended services that were literally meant to "scare the hell out of you." The speaker would paint such a terrifying picture of hell that you would never, ever, want to go there.

There is some value in this approach, as far as it goes. Certainly, the fear of a place filled with wailing, gnashing of teeth, and constant repetition of Barry Manilow's greatest hits is a powerful motivator. But we want to do more than fear eternal pain and misery; we want to turn our eyes to God and love him. We want to focus on what he has done for us and the inconceivable opportunities he has extended to us. Avoiding hell is good, but heaven is the prize.

So what can we know about heaven? We do know that, in some sense, heaven is a place. It has to be since Divine Revelation tells us that there are at least two bodies in heaven — Jesus's and Mary's.

But there are also many souls in heaven awaiting their bodies. The *Catechism* states that when a person dies, they go to what's called their *particular* judgment (1021). Everything we have done is judged right then by God, and the decision regarding where we are going to spend eternity happens at that moment. There are no second chances. No mulligans. We're taking the eternal elevator either up or down.

Even if God deems us worthy to spend eternity with him, we may still have to make a stop on the purgatory floor "so as to achieve the holiness necessary to enter the joy of heaven" (CCC 1030). As C. S. Lewis wrote:

> Our souls demand purgatory, don't they? Would it not break the heart if God said to us, "It is true, my son, that your breath smells and your rags drip with mud and slime, but we are charitable here and no one will upbraid you with these things, nor draw away from you. Enter into the joy"?
>
> Should we not reply, "With submission, sir, and if there is no objection, I'd rather be cleaned first."
>
> "It may hurt, you know" –
>
> "Even so, sir."[36]

When we are cleansed, our souls go to our final place, the place of eternal bliss where we join the angels and other saints who have gone before us.

But if you were to die right now, only your soul would go to heaven. At the end of time, there will come a final or last judgment for the whole world. The *Catechism* tells us that this is "the hour when all who are in the tombs will hear [the Son of man's] voice and come forth, those who have done good, to the resurrection of life, and those who have done evil, to the resurrection of judgment (Jn 5:28-29)" (1038).

So what's this resurrection all about? God made us a union of body and soul. That means that heaven isn't a place that we go to escape our bodies so we can somehow be "free." At the end of time we are going to get these carcasses back. Only this time, we'll get glorified bodies. Biceps will bulge, wrinkles will disappear, and the follicly challenged will once again boast Fabio-esque locks. Or something like that.

"A New Heaven and a New Earth"

Creation itself is related to this idea of our new glorified bodies. In the book of Genesis we find the description of how God created the universe, the heavens and the earth. That's how it all starts. Then at the end of the Bible, in the Book of Revelation, we read about "a *new* heaven and a *new* earth" (italics mine) that comes after the "first heaven and the first earth had passed away" (21:1).

This brings up an interesting point. While on the one hand heaven is beyond anything we can imagine, on the other hand Scripture and Tradition seem to tell us that it isn't something utterly unknown to us. It is a transformed and glorified version of what we now have. Genesis tells us that the heavens and earth God originally created were "very good" (1:31), but what we're going to get is "a new heaven and a new earth" that are even better. Not just Earth 2.0, but a whole new operating system.

A good place to observe this kind of transformation

is in the person of Christ. After he rose from the dead he appeared to Mary Magdalene in the garden. She doesn't recognize him at first, but then does. A similar encounter happens with the two disciples on the road to Emmaus that same Easter Sunday. He walks and talks with them for a while, but they don't know who he is even though presumably they had spent a good deal of time with him. They finally recognize him in the "breaking of the bread" (Lk 24:35), when Christ presides over what is essentially the second celebration of the Eucharist. Then he vanishes from their sight.

The two disciples roll back to Jerusalem lickety-split to tell the Eleven what had happened. And as they're describing it, Jesus reappears right in front of them. They freak out a bit, but he says to them, "See my hands and my feet, that it is I myself; handle me, and see; for a spirit has not flesh and bones as you see that I have" (Lk 24:39). He's showing them he's not a ghost. Sure, he can do some pretty nifty new tricks like walking through walls and disappearing at will, but he still has a body. He even asks them if they have anything to eat, so they give him some fish.

The point I want to emphasize is that Jesus Christ became, and remains, a flesh-and-blood man. He joined humanity to his divinity, transforming and glorifying it. This is a clue regarding what heaven will be like.

Lumen Gentium tells us that the "human race as well as the entire world, which is intimately related to man and attains to its end through him, will be perfectly reestablished in Christ" (48). In other words, the visible universe doesn't simply cease to exist at the end of time. It will be renewed, "transformed, 'so that the world itself, restored to its original state, facing no further obstacles, should be at the service of the just,' sharing their glorification in the risen Jesus Christ (St. Irenaeus, *Adv. Haeres.* 5,32,1: PG 7/2, 210)" (CCC 1047).

So the world we know is going to be transformed and glorified just as we will be, just as Christ was. It "will be set free from its bondage to decay" (CCC 1046).

If all of creation is to be "renewed" or "perfectly re-established in Christ," that means that the world as it is offers us at least a glimpse of what might be to come. Human experience teaches us this truth, as well. The beauty of this world and its effect upon us point us toward the infinite beauty of the Beatific Vision, which is our final destiny.

Heinz Hall

Let me give you an example from my own life of what I mean. Years ago, I was rushing up the stairs of Heinz Hall in Pittsburgh on a double date with my stunningly beautiful girlfriend. I mean this girl was drop-dead gorgeous. (She still is, and, yes, I married her.) Anyway, we were there to listen to the Pittsburgh symphony orchestra perform something or other. To be honest, I didn't know what was on the program. I had a mild interest in the music, but I was really there because of Veronica.

I love it now, but back then classical music wasn't

my favorite by any stretch. I found it a bit boring, especially compared with the 1980s pop and new wave I had been raised on. I wasn't even remotely open to the fact that some dead German or Russian guy's music could really compare to the glorious synthesizers of bands like Echo and the Bunnymen, the Psychedelic Furs, or Flock of Seagulls. (Those men were geniuses ... and hair connoisseurs.)

Be that as it may, I was frustrated because we were running late, and my fears of missing the first part were realized when we were held back from taking our seats as the first piece began. The iPhone had not yet been invented, so I glanced down at the program because I'd always found reading it a good way to distract myself during long nights at the symphony. (I would have brought a book to read, but I was told you were supposed to look like you were actually listening.)

Glancing from the program to the other patrons to the giant chandelier (what if that thing fell?), I was looking for anything to distract me from the inevitable boredom, and so I was totally unprepared for what happened next.

As soon as the first notes of the opening movement floated over the hall, I was frozen. I was completely captured and mesmerized by a melodic beauty I had never experienced before (not even in the greatest hits of the Thompson Twins). For the next few minutes I felt raptured out of myself, lost in the heavenly strains of Ralph Vaughn Williams's *Fantasia on a Theme by Thomas Tallis*.

I had never heard of Vaughn Williams, but his music

moved me almost to the point of tears. It made me long for something I couldn't quite wrap my emotions around or verbalize. I was completely lost in the moment. I could have stood there all night and listened to the fluid crescendos that flowed and rolled like huge waves in deep water. I was severely disappointed when it was over. Once planted in my velour-encrusted seat, all I could think about was that beautiful music.

What I didn't expect is that the whole experience was painful in a way. It was painful because it was a beauty I couldn't have. Painful because it was there, but only as a shadow is there and not a real person. And the worst part was, I couldn't recreate it. Not long after I attended this symphony, I tracked down and purchased the music. It was still beautiful, and it still moved me, but it didn't captivate me quite the way it had that night in Pittsburgh.

I learned an important lesson from this: You can't grasp beauty and fully possess it here. It's merely a foretaste of what is to come. C. S. Lewis describes the exact phenomenon I experienced: "The book or the music in which we thought the beauty was located will betray us if we trust to them; it was not in them, it only came through them, and what came through them was longing."[37]

The twentieth-century German Catholic philosopher Josef Pieper put it this way: "He who submits properly to the encounter with beauty will be given the sight and taste not of fulfillment, but of a promise, that in our bodily existence cannot be fulfilled."[38] This is why, when we are moved by something beautiful, we are never fully satisfied.

We go back and try to do it again to relive the experience, but it fulfills even less.

Beauty Opens Us to God

Even so, the beautiful things of this earth are important because they open us up to the beauty of God, the transcendent beauty of heaven. Earthly beauty is a kind of link to God, who is truth, beauty, and goodness. We hear a lot about truth and goodness, but our utilitarian culture has relegated true beauty to the back burner. I think this is especially true in the United States, where we build strip malls and box stores. Convenient? Yes. Beautiful? Not so much.

Our culture even goes so far as to negate natural beauty in parks through modern public "art." You know, those often hideous pieces of twisted metal. (Really? My taxes paid for a giant broken blender?) Even worse, many of our churches have been stripped of their beauty and no longer lead us through our senses to God. The fact is, my friends, real beauty matters.

The great theologian Hans Urs von Balthasar (whose very name almost demands we listen) said that whoever sneers at beauty "as if she were the ornament of a bourgeois past — whether he admits it or not — can no longer pray and will no longer be able to love."[39] Of course, this makes perfect sense. If God is the Beatific Vision, then beauty must matter. It is essential to our worship, and to our lives in general, because it's ordered to God.

Today, however, we face a problem: we can't declare something to be objectively beautiful or ugly without someone attacking us. ("What do you mean? That giant blender doesn't look broken to me!") Unfortunately, we live in a world full of Pontius Pilates, where truth has been almost completely relativized. For most, beauty is only "in the eye of the beholder."

To be sure, there is some truth to that. Certainly there is room for different tastes among people. Some people prefer vanilla ice cream and some chocolate. (I'm all about pistachio gelato.) But at some level there exists objective beauty. All of us recognize a burnt-orange sunset over the gently rolling waves of an ocean as beautiful. But how many of us are captivated by the clumps of lint pulled out of a dryer? You know, the kind that you have to lick your finger to get out — and then your finger is wet and you can't get the lint off. Not so lovely.

Ultimately, beauty is objective because it comes from God, the source and essence of beauty. Sin can never be beautiful; but truth is, goodness is. All three — truth, beauty, and goodness — have their origin in God and are the divine threads woven into the tapestry of this world. You can't underestimate the power of real beauty to influence conversion, either. I once met a successful Wall Street executive who had more money than he knew what to do with and so he started to buy a lot of art.

One day he bought a gorgeous painting of a mother and her child. He hung it on his wall among all his other paintings, but he kept coming back to it. Out of all his art, this particular piece captured him. He decided to find out the background of its subjects, little knowing that this picture of mother and child was a picture of *the* Mother and *the* Child, Mary and Jesus. Eventually, this painting effected his conversion, and he is now a faithful Catholic.

What's interesting about his conversion is that even though he wasn't actively seeking truth, it found him. It overcame him. There is no defense against beauty! Not even reason can stop it. Beauty goes around it like flowing water around a river rock.

Even so, the beautiful things of this world are but a promise. That's why we often experience joy and pain simultaneously when something truly beautiful moves us. It is a kind of bittersweetness that author Sheldon Vanauken calls "the pain of beauty."[40] It's the sweet sorrow of the here and now, but also of the not yet.

I'd be surprised if you haven't had an experience similar to mine at the symphony or to that of the gentleman with the painting. Maybe instead of music or a painting, it was the beauty of something in nature, or in another person, that overwhelmed you. Taken in by the beauty, you were taken out of yourself. It happens to people all the time, a hint of the glorious beauty for which we were all created — the Beatific Vision. We long for something we can't have in this life. Heaven is our beautiful end.

Bored to Death

While heaven is our end, sometimes when we talk about it, we're less than compelling. Philosopher and author Peter Kreeft points out that most of us are a bit vexed by theologians who theologize about staring at God forever, or by philosophers who philosophize about the perfections of God. For sure, these kinds of articulations are good and necessary, but they don't work for most of us. In fact, Kreeft says, these abstract descriptions can leave us cold or indifferent. He couldn't be more right. We humans relate to things through our senses, not just through abstract thinking.

The result, tragically, is that we make heaven sound a little boring. Perhaps you've caught yourself thinking: "I know we're all supposed to be trying to get to heaven, but it doesn't really sound as good as it's cracked up to be. Gold streets seem gaudy, and crowns and jewels don't really work with my favorite jeans. This kind of heaven just isn't doing it for me. And anyway, earth is full of terrific stuff, so I'd kind of like to stick around down here." Have you ever had those thoughts? Except for the jewels (which I've never worn and don't plan to), I have, too.

Billy Joel captures the attitude of a lot of people these days in his song "Only the Good Die Young" when he acknowledges that there might be a heaven, that it's supposed to be better than this present life — but he doesn't believe it is. He'd rather be with sinners than saints, he says, because "sinners are much more fun."

No wonder people don't get too excited about eternity. Consider the way in which popular culture describes our eternal abode. It's all kitsch! Who wants to sit on a cloud with a half-naked cherub strumming a harp? Forget that!

Wouldn't it be more fun to go skiing on a stellar slope in the Alps? How about surfing huge waves in Hawaii and then hanging out to watch the setting sun with our toes in the sand? Yes! Compared to the standard description of heaven, earth is certainly more fun.

And there's a reason for that. God made the Grand Canyon, Niagara Falls, and the Pacific Ocean. He made wild stallions, dolphins, and soaring eagles. He paints dry, desert sunsets over New Mexico and orchestrates symphonies of thunder and lightning that rattle the Rockies. Creation is a glorious place.

This God who created the beauty of this world is the same God who has prepared the inconceivable bliss of eternity, a "new heavens and a new earth" (Is 65:17). And the beauty of this world leads us to hope for the ecstasy of the life to come.

But as we discussed in the previous chapter, we all know from experience that the pleasures, ecstasies, and beauty of this world never really satisfy. Christmas always disappointed me when I was a kid, partly because my priorities were way off. Like most children, I wasn't focused on the miracle of Christ's birth. But I was also disappointed because no gifts ever really satisfied me — with the possible exception of the sweetest light-blue linen blazer that looked exactly like Don Johnson's on *Miami Vice*, a gift from my parents in 1985. But other than that jacket, which is long gone, no other gifts provided lasting satisfaction.

All of us have a longing for, an aching need for the infinite that can't be satisfied by the material goods of this earth or even by human relationships. The most in-love couple in the world eventually realizes that, ultimately, they can't satisfy each other. Their union will always be, in a sense, incomplete.

I'm certainly not trying to denigrate the beauty and depth of human relationships. Far from it. We are made to be in communion with other people. And this deep desire we have for union with those we love is important. In fact, it's yet another clue to the happiness we'll achieve in heaven.

Reunited and It Feels So Good

Perhaps the greatest promise of heaven is that one day we'll be reunited with those we have lost. I would even go so far as to say that, in a way, the death of someone near to you is one of the greatest arguments for the existence of heaven.

When my mother passed away a few years ago, I had a strange and in some ways infuriating experience. Mom was the center of our family, a true matriarch. When she finally succumbed to cancer, her death left a gaping hole in my world. Something that should not have been lost was suddenly gone. Here's the infuriating part. Even though my world stopped, the rest of the world kept right on going. Radios still blared insipid music and inane commercials. Stores kept selling. People drove here and there. The world simply moved on while mine had come to a screeching halt. I wanted to scream at everyone, "Don't you realize what's happened? She's gone!"

If you've lost a loved one, maybe you've had this same experience. What do you do with this? People are not meant to suddenly disappear. You might be unhappy when your TV breaks or when you chip a plate and must throw it away, but it's an altogether different story when a person dies. This is not the way it is supposed to be. And yet, the universe doesn't play favorites. Every day some people are born and some people die. This is the human condition.

The beautiful thing, the consoling thing, is that heaven holds the secure hope that our loved ones who have died are not gone forever. In fact, Lord willing, they're there right now waiting for us, and one day we will be reunited with them. I will be able to hug my mom again. I will meet the children my wife and I lost before they were born. I'll see long-lost friends. We will all truly be reunited in a deeper way than we ever experienced on earth. And this directs us again back to beauty.

United to Beauty

C. S. Lewis points out that as humans "we do not want merely to see beauty. We want something else which can hardly be put into words — to be united with the beauty we see, to pass into it, to receive it into ourselves, to bathe in it, to become part of it."[41]

That's probably why merely looking at beautiful things like mountains or oceans eventually frustrates me. Have you ever felt like that? I want more than just to look. I want to be a part of them, to be in them. I want to ski or climb the mountain. I want to surf on or dive into the ocean. I don't want to just look at my beautiful wife. I want to be one with her. It's the same with many of our relationships. Why else would parents plant their faces on babbies's tummies and blow so as to send them into gales of giggles? It's because they're so ridiculously adorable that it's the only way you know how to physically express your love for them, to be close to them.

Of course, at some point the day arrives when your children grow up. All parents eventually reach the stage where if they tried to blow on their children's tummies the state would intervene. Truth be told, it's kind of a drag when your children are no longer kids. I've never met a young(ish) parent who didn't lament the fact that their children were getting too big, too fast. If I had a nickel for every time some older parent or grandparent told me to enjoy the time when my kids are little, I wouldn't have to worry about how to pay for their college education.

Of course, they're right. My oldest is barely into double digits, and I already feel it. I don't want her to stop playing with dolls. I don't want her to stop holding my hand when we walk down the street. And I certainly don't want to give her the keys to my car! We parents mourn the fact that we can't continue to experience our babies in all of their beautiful, large-eyed chubbiness or the joy of their "first times," such as sitting up, crawling, and spitting up on strangers.

It almost makes me cry to think there will be a day when I won't have a perfect, sleeping baby to gaze upon in the crib next to my bed. (It makes me weep bitterly when they migrate into my bed at 2:00 a.m.) I think this is why God created grandparents. They get to go through it all again, but at a slower pace. They can enjoy it more, especially the part about handing the baby back to their son or daughter and saying, "I think she needs to be changed."

We can't escape the fact that the passage of time kills us, figuratively and literally. We can't slow it down, though we're constantly trying to save it. It slips through our grasp like water through a closed fist. Time flies. The clock keeps ticking. We can't stop it and it drives us nuts — because we were made for timelessness.

The Time of Our Life

But this is another comforting thing about heaven — it includes all of time. All the beautiful experiences of this life aren't left behind permanently: my wedding, the births of my children, the first time I put on that blue linen Don Johnson jacket, whatever. Heaven includes the joy and security of the past and the happy hope of all things new.

In his book *A Severe Mercy*, about his life with his wife and her untimely death, Sheldon Vanauken draws an analogy between how we will experience time in heaven and reading a book like David Copperfield which spans many years. In heaven, he muses, we'll be able to go back to different points in life and see that person at that point in time, just as you can turn back to a particular chapter and read about David Copperfield at a particular point in his life.

I like to think of it more as a photo album where you can turn back and look at particular images of a person's life. Of course, in heaven, you won't have to rely on images because you'll know the whole person — "fully understood," as Saint Paul says (1 Cor 13:12).

Peter Kreeft, who has written several excellent books about heaven, makes an interesting point about this nostalgia for the past that we all experience, the "good old days." He says that in a sense, humanity is longing for Eden, our lost identity, our likeness to God.[42] We long for home, and it is a direction that goes back in nostalgia, but also forward in hope to our heavenly home.

Of course, we can't go back in this life. Your childhood home may hold wonderful memories, and it's fun to drive by your old house after you've moved, but it's probably better not to go in. You might freak if you saw what they did with your old room. (What? My sailing-ships wallpaper wasn't good enough for you?)

As fun as it is to see that old house, most of us don't move back in (unless we received a liberal-arts education and can't find a job). Not even Adam and Eve were allowed back in the garden after they sinned. We must go forward in hope with the knowledge that once we're in eternity, all of time will be opened to us.

Heaven as Homecoming

Still, we all maintain a deep-seated need for home. Every man, says Blessed John Henry Newman, "wants a center on which to place his thoughts and affections, a secret dwelling-place which may soothe him after the troubles of the world."[43] That's why it's such a great feeling to come back home after a trip.

Perhaps the lack of this comforting sanctuary is what Jesus was referencing when he said, "Foxes have holes, and birds of the air have nests; but the Son of man has nowhere to lay his head" (Lk 9:58). Jesus moved from town to town preaching the kingdom of God and experiencing a kind of homelessness in his humanity. Of course, later, he tells us that he is going back to the Father to prepare a place for us in his Father's house, "that where I am you may be also" (Jn 14:3).

Ultimately, heaven is our homecoming. It's the home we were made for, the place where we can be what we were made to be. Where we will know all and be fully known. Where we'll have everything we ever longed for and more. No more pain, no more tears, no more sadness — inconceivable joy for ever and ever and ever and ever. This is our final, beautiful end.

The Beauty of Sainthood

But at the end of the day, heaven isn't simply a place; it's a person. In fact, it's Three Persons. In heaven, we will see God face-to-face — this Beatific Vision is the heart of heaven. The person who is united most completely to God on earth is the person who reveals the beauty of God and the hope of heaven to the rest of us. That's why the most beautiful thing on earth isn't a snowcapped mountain or the midnight moon shining on the ocean; it's a saint.

Saints have totally conformed themselves to Christ and so reflect his beauty, though it's a beauty this world doesn't often recognize. Why? Because the beauty of God on earth is found in the portrait of a bloody and beaten savior who hung on the cross for humanity. This perfect image of divine beauty can be realized only in self-denial, self-offering, self-death — the path chosen by the saints.

Christ spells out this path for us in his Sermon on the Mount, particularly in the beatitudes, which give the blueprint for a holy life.

The Beatitudes

Most modern translations of the Sermon on the Mount use the word "blessed" at the beginning of each of the beatitudes, but the Church Fathers preferred the term "happy."[44] They preferred happy because ultimately, the beatitudes are ordered to happiness.

Happy are "the poor in spirit, for theirs is the kingdom of heaven." Happy are "those who mourn," "the meek," those who "hunger and thirst for righteousness," "the merciful," "the pure in heart," "the peacemakers," the "persecuted." You're even supposed to be happy "when men revile you and persecute you and utter all kinds of evil against you falsely on [Christ's] account. Rejoice and be glad." Why? For "your reward is great in heaven" (Mt 5:3-12).

The Sermon on the Mount is a kind of summary of

the whole Gospel of Christ. And the beatitudes, embedded within the Sermon, have been described as a summary of the Sermon on the Mount.[45] They basically tell us how to be happy, both now and in eternity. And notice that all of them are ordered to the kingdom of heaven, which is the phrase after the first and last beatitude.

I encourage you to read them and ponder them in prayer, because the beatitudes take the hardships we experience in this world (poverty, sorrow, hunger, persecution) along with attributes that seem impossible (meekness, mercy, purity, peace) and make them the paradoxical path to heaven.

The beatitudes turn the priorities of this world upside down. Only in Christ can the poor, the afflicted, and the persecuted be truly happy. Only through Christ can we be meek, merciful, and pure in heart. The beatitudes offer us hope for today, as well as for the future. They are the keys to the kingdom of heaven. They lead us to the Beatific Vision of God.

The late Servais Pinkaers, a Catholic priest and theologian, said that the beatitudes and the whole of the Sermon on the Mount reveal to us the "spiritual face of Christ."[46] This idea perhaps sheds a little more light on what Christ meant when he said that "the eye is the lamp of the body. So, if your eye is sound, your whole body will be full of light; but if your eye is not sound, your whole body will be full of darkness" (Mt 6:22-23). Sin casts us into the shadows. It clouds our vision of God. It's like wearing dark sunglasses in a windowless basement. You're left groping for the stairway that leads up to the light.

We can't see God unless our vision is pure. And we must remember that our eyes are actually ordered to the Beatific Vision — that's what they will ultimately gaze upon. And so what we look upon now matters. We must guard our gaze because there is much in this world that is an assault on the beauty of God. Paul reminds us to focus on "whatever is true, whatever is honorable, whatever is just, whatever is pure, whatever is lovely, whatever is gracious" (Phil 4:8).

Sin, in fact, can lead people to develop objectively bad taste. (And I don't just mean bad clothing decisions such as dark socks with tennis shoes.) Sin is one of the reasons some people think objectively ugly things are beautiful. Their minds have been darkened by perversity, by the world, and they no longer recognize true beauty. You want to know why there are people in this world who think a toilet bowl qualifies as "art" in an art museum? Because "the fascination of wickedness obscures what is good" (Wis 4:12).

Proving Ground

At the end of the day, we might not know exactly what awaits us in heaven, but we can be sure that it is supremely beautiful. The glories of this world, while beautiful in themselves, are but a shadow of this unsurpassed glory. "Now we see in a mirror dimly," as Saint Paul says (1 Cor 13:12).

Heaven is our destiny. We are bound for limitless

beauty, created for unimaginable glory. Even so, we can't forget that this world is our proving ground. Ask yourself on a daily basis if you are living so as to add or detract from divine beauty. Our goal should be to let go of this world and let the Great Artist mold us and shape us back into his magnificent likeness. God is beauty. Heaven is our beautiful end. Together in Christ, we should live beautiful lives now, so as to live beautifully forever.

Of course, creating a beautiful life takes commitment and time, not to mention some God-given grace and talent. Let's now turn our focus to the tools of the heavenly trade.

CHAPTER 7

OUR DAILY BREAD

THE THING ABOUT HEAVEN IS THAT IT'S NOT EARTH — and that means what we consider important here isn't so important there. As earthlings still making our way toward our final destiny, we have a tendency to exalt attributes — athletic prowess, intellectual gifts, non-receding hairlines — that have little value beyond the here and now.

Natural talents and abilities are nothing to demean, of course, because "every good and perfect gift is from above" (Jas 1:17). Many of the saints, in fact, were naturally gifted academically, athletically, or in business — and all excelled in holiness. But some of the saints seemed to excel *only* in holiness. In short, they apparently had no other natural gifts, at least none that caught the eye. This was true of Saint John Vianney, the Curé of Ars, a poster child for the idea that in Christ we are strong in our weakness (see 1 Cor 12:9). But in his love for God and the Church — particularly the Eucharist — he shows us the things that really matter in this life.

A Talent for Holiness

John Vianney grew up in an impoverished farming family during the French Revolution and the topsy-turvy era of Napoleon that followed. Classrooms were as foreign to John as the English — academically speaking, he was the bottom of the barrel. This was a severe handicap because John wanted to be a priest, and the priesthood and academic prowess went hand-in-hand. His Latin was terrible, and philosophy was his bane. Once, when John was attending classes to prepare to enter the seminary, a much younger student actually punched him because John couldn't come up with the answer to a question.[47] To say that his future as a priest was uncertain would be a strong understatement at best.

As shocking as it now seems, the patron saint of parish priests was almost not ordained. When he finally did receive holy orders, this man who would eventually spend three-quarters of his life in a confessional was not allowed to hear confessions because of his academic record.[48] But what Vianney lacked in intellectual rigor, he made up for in humility. Upon being punched by the younger student, for example, he dropped to his knees, apologizing for his "poor head."

The future saint made it through pre-seminary studies only because of the unflagging help of his mentor, Father Charles Balley, who recognized John's holiness. When Vianney went on to the minor seminary for further study, however, it was like a lamb to the slaughter. The faculty sent him packing after six months with the lowest grade possible. In fact, "it would have been lower," said one biographer, "but there was no lower grade, so they drew a line through it."[49] Ouch!

Poor Vianney sank into despair, but Father Balley refused to give up. Convinced Vianney had a vocation, he was able to present him for examinations again. After one false start, the future Curé passed and went on to be ordained. It was a miracle. If France had been at peace and not in great need of priests, Saint John Vianney would probably never have reached his goal. But because everything is in God's hands, Vianney "slipped into history when history was looking the other way."[50]

No Small Saint

The story of the Curé of Ars is a great reminder that often the world doesn't know "jack." Not long after becoming a Catholic I had the opportunity to travel to the little French town of Ars. I was visiting a friend who was studying in a seminary there. Cold, tired, and relatively ignorant about Catholic heroes, I agreed to visit the church of the Curé, but with an interest bordering on indifference. What I encountered, however, was unforgettable.

John Vianney was a warrior for Christ. I saw where he heard confessions day after day, reading souls like an open book for eighteen hours in a row. I saw the burn marks on his bed frame from one of the numerous times the devil tried to intimidate him. I even saw his barely five-foot-tall incorrupt body! (No doubt he was chosen last for pickup hoops.)

To be honest, I wasn't sure what to do with all of this at first, but I have a better appreciation now. How can you not be awestruck by a priest who established a school and orphanage for needy girls in the area, selling his possessions one by one in order to provide for them and their teachers? Once he even tried to pull out his own teeth when in jest someone offered him money for them. He would do anything for his spiritual children.

God loved this generous little priest, rewarding the prayers of the Curé with great miracles. Once, for example, the orphanage, which relied on donations and alms, was down to its final grains of wheat. Vianney, in an act of great faith, scraped together what he could and placed the little mound in front of a statue of Saint Francis Regis, a saint to whom Vianney attributed some of his help in becoming a priest. He gathered the young children in his care around the little shrine and prayed. When the teacher sent to gather the remaining wheat from the attic opened the door, she was astonished to find grain flowing past her down the stairs. The large attic was so full they wondered how it didn't collapse. This turned out to be the first recognized miracle for the future saint.

As with so many other saints, it was the basics that gave Vianney such faith and trust in Our Lord: Mass, confession, and prayer. He didn't fool around. When asked how best to get to God, he replied, "Quite straight, like a cannonball."[51] And he knew the straightest way to God is through the sacraments. "Put all the good works in the world against one Communion well made," said the Curé, "and they are like a speck of dust beside a mountain."

Our Daily Bread

Growing up as a pastor's kid, I was not unacquainted with the insides of church buildings. There were Sunday morning and Sunday evening services, Wednesday night services, potluck dinners, youth-group activities, and other organizations such as choirs and AWANA (imagine Christian Boy Scouts without knives and camping — bummer, I know). If I wasn't at home or school, odds were I was at church.

Regardless, I was more than a little shocked to discover that many Catholics go to Mass every day. Even more shocking was that every Mass was essentially the same as the day before. There were no gimmicks. And contrary to popular opinion, daily Mass is not solely populated by little old ladies adorned with so many Miraculous Medals and rosaries that they look like they just received a Catholic Mr. T starter kit. (Be advised — they tend to be the holiest people on the planet.) In fact, at my alma mater, Franciscan University, the multiple Masses each day are often standing-room only. It's been that way for a long time.

I guess I shouldn't have been surprised when I encountered so many people spending thirty to forty-five minutes a day in church. It's kind of a no-brainer when you think about it. After all, God is there. That's what it boils down to. Every day a priest goes to the altar and makes Christ available — Body and Blood, Soul and Divinity — to every Catholic, and it happens all over the world.

Stop and think about that. Almighty God, the Creator of the universe, the God who gave us breath and holds our very being in existence, offers himself to us every day. The question that's begging to be asked is whether or not we're going to meet him as often as possible. What kind of an effort are we making?

Let's put this in perspective. Imagine if you were the greatest doctor in the world, knew the answer to every medical problem, and could heal any disease. You had offices in every neighborhood around the world, they were open every day, and your services were free. Do you think you would ever have any downtime? Of course not. Your offices would be packed.

You already know where I'm going with this, but I find the situation incredibly vexing: Why are there so many Catholics who don't go to Mass as often as possible? Instead of merely gaining relief from temporary physical maladies from a fictional super-doctor, we have the opportunity to meet with the God of the universe, who wants to give us peace, joy, happiness, healing — everything he's got, forever!

None of us should ever settle for the minimum. Get to confession as often as necessary, and go to Mass as often as you possibly can. The Sunday obligation is just that, an obligation. It's the low bar. But love isn't about obligation. We should be excited to commune with Our Lord just as we do with our loved ones here on earth. He wants nothing more than to give himself to us.

Jesus taught us to ask the Father for "our daily bread." Following his lead, Saint Ambrose asks a very pointed question: "If it is 'daily' bread, then why do you take it so infrequently? Take daily what will help you daily. And live so that you deserve to receive it daily. He who does not deserve to receive it daily does not deserve to receive it once a year."[52]

Look, I realize it's not always easy to get to daily Mass. If you simply can't make that work with your schedule, then try to make a spiritual communion with Our Lord every day. Take a few minutes and read the Scripture readings for that day. Do whatever you can to join yourself to the mysteries that are celebrated in the Eucharistic liturgy.

Take a hard look at your daily activities, however, to see if there are things you can change in order to make more frequent Mass attendance possible. In other words, don't let your worldly schedule take precedence. I realize this can entail a major life change. It's a big commitment. I get it. My schedule is just as demanding as the next guy's. I have a wife, four kids (and counting), a job, home repairs, car repairs, ballet classes (for my *girls*!), soccer games, yada, yada, yada. Life is demanding.

On the other hand, think about the last time you were head over heels in love. And I don't mean with a car or a pair of shoes, I mean with a flesh-and-blood person. A lot of you probably married that person. Or maybe you're in the midst of dating that guy or girl right now.

Highway Love

When you're in love with someone, you want to be with them all the time. When I first started dating my wife,

I lived in Chicago and she lived in Steubenville, Ohio. Every couple of weeks, I would finish up a fifty-five-hour work week, get in my car, and fight rush-hour traffic for an hour just for the privilege of driving another seven hours on what has to be one of the most boring roads in America, Interstate 80. I'd spend Saturday and half of Sunday with her and then drive the seven or eight hours back. A couple of weeks later I'd do it again. And then again.

The travel was a grind. That being said, unless I was yelling at someone for cutting me off or looking for an opportunity to cut someone else off, I was generally smiling. It was all worth it because I was in love.

When I wasn't traveling to see her, I would compose long, poetic e-mails, or spend hours every night on the phone with her. I finally moved to Steubenville because I couldn't stand to live apart from her.

Many of you have probably done similar things. In the early days of dating, when you were all twitterpated, maybe you got up very early just to drive to your love's car and leave a note or a flower. Perhaps you'd stay up late watching a movie together (stuff you'd *never* watch alone), knowing you would be exhausted in the morning. It didn't matter. You were in *love*, and you were willing to make sacrifices for the relationship.

Well, you know what? That's the kind of relationship that God wants to have with us. He wants us to make him a priority, *the* priority. With so much going on in our lives, it's easy to forget who and what are most important, so here's a suggestion. When you think it's too much of a sacrifice to make it to an early morning or evening Mass, grab a crucifix and look at it. Stare at it. Jesus was beaten to a bloody pulp and then nailed to a cross. And that was only the culmination of the sacrifice he made for you. His suffering love started long before that. So what are you willing to do for him?

If you're thinking that I'm trying to make you feel guilty, you're right! Sometimes guilt is good. But realize that at the end of the day it's not about fear and guilt; *it's about love*.

God didn't just say he loves us more than we can possibly imagine; he acted on it. He put his money where his mouth is. And he continues to offer himself to us on a moment-by-moment basis. All we have to do is respond. We *must* respond! We have to get to confession and then to Mass as often as we can. Without the grace that Christ offers us in the sacraments we can't be the people we ought to be.

Word and Deed

If we're going to evangelize the world, we must start with ourselves. People are tired of being told how they're supposed to live; they want someone to show them, to lead them. That's why the saints rocked. They taught by word and deed. And their deeds started with the sacraments, especially the Eucharist, because "the liturgy is the summit toward which the activity of the Church is directed."[53] Everything in this life, everything in *our* life, should revolve around the Mass. The Eucharist is the "medicine of immortality."[54] It is "the source and summit of the Christian life."[55] It's everything!

In fact, Blessed John Paul II declared that the New Evangelization is centered on the Eucharist. He said:

> [It's] a "missionary" sacrament not only because the grace of mission flows from it, but also because it contains in itself the principle and eternal source of salvation for all. The celebration of the Eucharistic sacrifice is therefore the most effective missionary act that the ecclesial community can perform in the history of the world.[56]

At the end of every Eucharistic celebration the priest gives us a missionary mandate to "Go!" We're supposed to proclaim to the world the joy of our Jesus encounter. The Eucharist is a missionary event because every time it is celebrated we "proclaim the Lord's death until he comes" (1 Cor 11:26).

And though we're supposed to go and proclaim to the world what God has done, conversion happens first in us. We must be transformed in order to help God transform others. Everything we do emanates from Jesus, whom we receive in the Eucharist. That's why Saint Bernadette Soubirous said, our "soul should be occupied with one thought alone: preparing [our] heart to be God's dwelling place."[57]

Of course, that preparation can take place in different ways, but one of the most important means we have to prepare ourselves for the Lord — one neglected by too many Catholics — is sacred Scripture.

CHAPTER 8

THE NEED TO READ

GROWING UP AS A PROTESTANT PASTOR'S KID, I was surrounded by Scripture. Our faith revolved around it. Armed
with the latest in cutting-edge, flannel-graph technology, our
Sunday school teachers taught us the great stories and led us
in games meant to drill as much Scripture into our noggins
as possible. After they finished with us, they herded us into
the main church building for yet more Scripture from our
pastor. In many ways, it was great formation. I learned a lot.
But it wasn't enough. There is far more.

While I still venerate the Bible as the inspired, iner-
rant Word of God (as does the Church), I've come to realize that our faith revolves around the Mass. As we noted
earlier, it's the "summit" of our activities as Catholics. It's
where heaven and earth kiss. In fact, the Mass is nothing
less than a participation in the liturgy of the angels and
the saints in heaven.[58]

We tend to associate the Mass only with the Eucharist, however, and that's a problem. It's the culmination of
the celebration, no doubt about it, but there are two parts
to the Mass: the Liturgy of the Word, followed by the
Liturgy of the Eucharist. We don't receive the Eucharist
until we have first been prepared by the Word. What is

proclaimed in Scripture is then actualized in the Eucharist. First we hear, then we receive.

Word and Sacrament

Jesus himself lays out this pattern in the story of the two disciples on the road to Emmaus that we looked at earlier (Lk 24:13-35). As he walked with them on the road "he interpreted to them in all the scriptures the things concerning himself" (v. 27). After he blew their minds with his Scripture teaching, they asked him to stay for dinner. At table "he took the bread and blessed, and broke it, and gave it to them" (v. 30). Just as at Mass, the disciples were first prepared with Scripture, and then Scripture led them into a celebration of the Eucharist.

The event in Emmaus follows the pattern of the Last Supper account that appears two chapters earlier in the Gospel of Luke and uses virtually the same language. Emmaus, then, was essentially the second celebration of the Mass, the second time "Christ was carried in his own hands," according to Saint Augustine.[59] On both occasions, Christ demonstrated the relationship between Word and sacrament. Scripture prepares us to receive Our Lord in the Eucharist.

There are two important points to consider here. First, Scripture is most at home in the Mass. The liturgy is its natural habitat. In fact, the Catholic Church formally defined the canon of Scripture in the late 300s particularly so that priests would know what books and letters to proclaim in the liturgy. Scripture, sacraments, and liturgy go together. Pope Benedict XVI declared that "Word and Eucharist are so deeply bound together that we cannot understand one without the other: the word of God sacramentally takes flesh in the event of the Eucharist."[60]

The second point is derived from the first. If Scripture best prepares us to receive Our Lord in the Eucharist, the "source and summit" of our faith, then we had better get to know the Bible (CCC 1324). Without it, our sacramental encounter with Christ can go only so deep. Remember, there is enough grace in one consecrated host to save the world. The only thing stopping it from saving us, is us.

Ignorance Is No Excuse

There's no way around the fact that if we don't read the Bible, we can't know Jesus. It's the only inspired book in the entire world that tells us all about him. And when I say "inspired," I don't mean that it was a good idea. I mean that the words of Scripture are the very words of God.

Saint Paul says that "all scripture is inspired by God" (2 Tm 3:16). The Greek word he uses for "inspired" in that verse is *theopneustos*, which literally means "God-breathed." As the *Catechism* states, God is "the principal author of Sacred Scripture" (304). What other book can make that claim? None. The Bible is God's own book, written about him. If we don't read it, he remains a stranger. "Ignorance of Scripture is ignorance of Christ," said Saint Jerome.

It's important to get to know him in the sacred page, but lots of Catholics currently sporting gray locks learned in the *Baltimore Catechism* that God created us not just to know him, but to love and serve him as well.[61] We "younger" folks need to learn this, too. We don't read the holy writ simply to gain knowledge, but so that it will influence and shape our actions. "When you open the Holy Gospel," said Saint Josemaría Escrivá, "think that what is written there — the words and deeds of Christ — is something that you should not only know, but live."[62]

Love Letters

Not many of us receive actual letters anymore, especially love letters. But for kick's sake, let's say you were all gooey in love with someone who lived far away. If a letter from that person arrived in your mailbox (or inbox, as it were), you'd tear it open immediately. The first time through you'd read it at lightning speed (looking for the mushy stuff), and then again and again more slowly, reveling in it.

Now imagine that you are getting personal notes from Almighty God, the Creator of the world, telling you how much he loves you and wants to save you. He wants to give you everything he's got and provide you with untold bliss for eternity. Would you leave those letters unopened? Of course not. But that's what the Bible is, God's love letter to you. Given that, it's shocking that some people treat Scripture like a piece of junk mail, tossed aside, never to be opened and read.

Shocking too, given widespread indifference to Scripture, is the fact that many of us know way too much about the most unimportant things. Speaking for myself, I would go so far as to say that my mind is a cesspool of pop culture and sports trivia, particularly from the glorious decade of new wave, neon, and Rubik's Cube. My ability to recall the name of an obscure '80s British band, or to remember a particular play from a 1984 *Monday Night Football* game sometimes frightens me. I can do it because I spent an inordinate amount of time in my youth listening to that music and watching those sports.

Imagine if you and I knew as much about the Bible as most Americans know about football (or the rest of the world knows about soccer). Fourth-century saint and Doctor of the Church John Chrysostom wondered along similar lines. Commenting on the pop culture of his day, he asked:

> Is it not strange that those who sit by the market can tell the names, and families, and cities of charioteers, and dancers, and the kinds of powers possessed by each, and can give exact account of the good or bad qualities of the very horses, but those who come hither [to the church] should know nothing of what is done here, but should be ignorant of the number even of the sacred Books?[63]

Indulge Me

The long and the short of it? Scripture is necessary if we want to grow in holiness and strive toward sainthood. It tells us how we can please the Father and be saved. Saint Augustine's massive conversion finally took off when he heard a child's voice chanting, "Take it and read; take it and read."[64]

At the time, Augustine was in a garden in an agony of indecision, wanting to be free of sin and become a Christian, but held back by the things of the world, particularly the call to chastity. When he heard the child's voice from a nearby house, he hesitated, trying to determine if the chant was part of a children's game. Unable to place it as such, he decided it was a divine command to open Scripture and read the first passage his eye fell upon. He picked up his Bible, opened at random, and read: "Not in reveling and drunkenness, not in debauchery and licentiousness, not in quarreling and jealousy. But put on the Lord Jesus Christ and make no provision for the flesh" (Rom 13:13-14). In that brief moment, all his "darkness of doubt" passed away.[65] The rest is holy history.

Take some time off from surfing the Web or watching television and start to read about the things that matter most. Learn the story of our faith. Get to know the biblical heroes and imitate them. Dive into the story of salvation history that is still being played out today. It's not just a story about people who have long since died, it's *your* story.[66]

If growing in knowledge of the deepest and most beautiful mysteries in the world isn't enough incentive to prompt you to read, I have some news for you. If you read the Bible for a mere thirty minutes a day, you can receive a plenary indulgence.[67] Just read, get to sacramental confession and the Eucharist within twenty days, pray for the Holy Father's intentions, and get rid of attachment to sin. Once that's accomplished — congratulations! You just scored a plenary indulgence.

Of course, the merits of an indulgence don't just apply to us, they can even be applied to the faithful departed. I don't know about you, but unloading the temporal punishment of sins by reading the best book in the world for half an hour sounds pretty good. I'm all about the fastest elevator possible out of purgatory, either for myself or someone else.

The point of the indulgence, of course, is to help us draw closer to Christ. The fact is, we can't fall in love with someone we don't know. Just so, we can't fall in love with Christ without reading his Word. And that leads us into the next piece of the puzzle in the art of learning to live as a Catholic — the role and importance of prayer.

CHAPTER 9

THE PRIMACY
OF PRAYER

As a Catholic, I've come to understand and appreciate as I hadn't before that Christ isn't merely looking to be our friend. He doesn't just want to be a buddy. Good thing, because I've got plenty of buddies. (Not that I wouldn't bump one of them off the couch to make room for Christ, mind you.)

Rather, he wants us to become his brothers and sisters. That's always his goal, to live in a familial relationship with us. Friendship isn't enough. That family relationship is established through the grace of the sacraments, but cultivated through prayer (see CCC 2558). A sacramental life devoid of prayer is like an exquisite meal with no utensils. You need both.

Most of us, however, aren't wondering *if* we should pray, but rather *how* we should raise our "mind and heart to God" in prayer (CCC 2559). We *want* to foster a relationship with God, and we recognize that prayer somehow will help us do that. Prayer helps us deal with this fallen world and come out perfect on the other side. It draws us closer to the Lord so we can tell him what's going on, make our needs known, offer up our sufferings, grow in holiness, and become more like him. All the saints trod the path of prayer, and we must too.

The Conversation Begins

But as important as prayer is, for many of us it's shrouded in mystery, like the ingredients in a hot dog. What exactly is prayer? For starters, it helps to know that it comes in different basic forms: blessing, adoration, petition, intercession, thanksgiving, and praise. More descriptively, the *Catechism* says that "prayer is the encounter of God's thirst with ours" (2560). Saint Thérèse of Lisieux, the Little Flower, says that "prayer is a surge of the heart; it is a simple look turned toward heaven, it is a cry of recognition and of love, embracing both trial and joy (St. Thérèse of Lisieux, *Manuscrits autobiographiques*, C 25r.)" (2558). It's where we encounter Christ, who constantly seeks us.

Note that when the Little Flower speaks of the heart, she's talking about that place deep inside ourselves to which we withdraw — our interior life. We might not think about it much, but each of us has an interior life. It's that conversation that takes place inside when we are alone with ourselves. Sometimes that conversation leads us to self-examination or reflection upon the important matters of life and how we're living life. But we also have to admit that there are often times when this conversation is self-centered in a bad way. It's easy to become consumed with ourselves and focus on our own needs and desires.

Prayer, however, changes our focus. Under the influence of grace, our interior conversation moves away from being self-centered and becomes a conversation with God. As our interior life is transformed and elevated, our gaze shifts outward and upward. This is the goal.

Until this happens we continue to satiate our desires with distractions. We keep trying to squash that still, small voice that continually tells us there is something more we haven't found yet: "The stuff you're feeding me isn't working. Give me more!" So we move from one distraction to the next in search of peace.

This self-seeking is a path that leads to death. And being the creative geniuses we are, we keep trying to find new ways — often sinful — to fill that hole that only a relationship with God can fill. Our soul was made for prayer — that conversation with the Other who made us.

Bowled Over

Obviously this isn't your ordinary conversation — it can pack a punch — so let's stop for a moment to consider the power of prayer. In prayer we encounter Almighty God, a fact that makes fervent prayer highly effective. Indeed, Saint James declares, "the prayer of a righteous man has great power in its effects" (Jas 5:16). Scripture is chock-full of stories that demonstrate this truth: Elijah asking for, and receiving, fire from heaven to crush the priests of Baal (1 Kgs 18); Hannah praying to conceive and then bearing Samuel (1 Sm 1:1—2:10); Peter praying for Tabitha, who then rose from the dead (Acts 9:36-42). Scripture makes it clear that prayer is powerful, but in my experience nothing explains the power of prayer quite like bowling.

When but a young, Protestant lad in high school, I knew only one Catholic family. Ironically, we met at a Calvinist high school in the Chicago suburbs and became fast friends. Two of the boys in the family were twins, replete with hair the color of a fiery sunset and Irish tempers to match. Well-catechized by their parents, they were just as ardently Catholic as I was Protestant. As such, we had some interesting "discussions" about the faith over the course of our high school and college years. And our private Thirty Years' War wasn't limited to words. We were men of action.

Not surprisingly, then, one fateful Friday night we found ourselves in a bowling alley. We were joined by another Protestant friend, who evened the odds of our battle. After selecting our heavy artillery from racks full of scuffed, polyurethane cannonballs, we declared war. It was to be Protestants versus Catholics in an all-out bowling melee for truth, justice, and the Reformation — or so I thought.

Supremely confident in my comparative bowling prowess (I had spent a few weeks in a sixth-grade league, after all), I settled in for an enjoyable evening comfortably clad in my multicolored footwear. But, alas, within this cacophonous, terribly tiled establishment I was to meet a cruel fate. Over the course of a mere half-hour I watched in disbelief as these upstart papists managed to put themselves in a position to actually win the game. We hit the tenth frame. If they somehow — impossibly (you've never seen them bowl) — achieved a strike, they would win.

Tossing aside fear like a spent match, the twin preparing to bowl confidently turned toward me and began to pray out loud. And not just any prayer — he was praying to Mary! "Hail Mary, full of grace ... " I seethed and grinned hideously at the same time, furious at his idolatry while rejoicing in his folly. No way would God honor that prayer.

By the time the tenth pin completed its lazy death spin, my smile had vanished and my head hung low in defeat. Not only did the twins know the power of prayer; they obviously knew more people to whom they could pray.

Mechanically Inclined

When it comes to prayer, however, many of us are dealing with a more fundamental problem than its power in relation to disastrous bowling outings. Instead, we're facing the hard fact that even if we do pray regularly, we treat the exercise as merely something to be ticked off our spiritual to-do list. There's no real vitality. On a broad level, this has something to do with the fact that, as we've seen, when Adam sinned, humanity lost its likeness to God. But "prayer," says the *Catechism*, "restores man to God's likeness and enables him to share in the power of God's love (cf. *Rom* 8:16-21)" (2572). How do we get there?

We already mentioned several stories about prayer in

Scripture, and there are many more. All the great figures of salvation history — Abraham, Jacob, Moses, David, Mary, and so many others — were people of prayer. The book of Psalms, much of which was written by David, is essentially a book of prayers. The Jerusalem Temple itself, the center of the Israelite religion, was a house of sacrifice and prayer (see CCC 2581).

Prayer permeated the lives of the Israelites, yet they messed up time and again. Too many of them never really entered into true worship of God. Catholics today, I think, face the same problem the Israelites faced: we know many forms of prayer, but we haven't had a conversion of heart that would transform the way we pray (see CCC 2581).

I shudder to think how many times I have droned mindlessly through an Our Father in Mass. How many Rosaries have I recited without any focus on the mysteries? I know I shouldn't, but sometimes I take solace in the fact that I'm not alone. I was attending Mass in Ireland a few years ago and heard an older lady blow through an entire Rosary in what seemed to be about ninety seconds. Her Irish accent was so thick and she was going so fast that I'm not sure even God understood her.

On the other hand, I remember praying a Rosary with a guy who thought a decade was actually supposed to last ten years. I impatiently stroked the beads, lamenting the fact that by the time it was over my best years would be behind me.

If we're not careful, there's no doubt that our Memorares, Rosaries, litanies, and so forth can become rote. I'm not saying these forms of prayer aren't important. Not at all! Catholic prayers are full of beauty and depth and often express things in a way we never could. In fact, you've no idea how happy I am to have such great "set" prayers. As a Protestant I had to come up with stuff on the fly. It was hard! Because we ran out of material so quickly, my buddies and I would fall back on certain phrases. But as Catholics, we have beautiful prayers always available to us. Even Jesus, as a good Jew, learned all the forms of prayer of his time. But he also shows us that prayer to the Father is just that — the prayer of the Son to his Father (see CCC 2599).

What Is Prayer?

Of course, it's easy to talk about prayer, but quite another actually to do it. Let's discuss it in concrete terms so that we can draw closer to God in prayer, receive his love, and fulfill the eternal destiny for which he created us.

For starters, prayer is not random. It can't be reduced, says the *Catechism*, to a "spontaneous ... interior impulse: in order to pray, one must have the will to pray" (2650). In other words, we have to decide to do it. We all know that we don't always feel like praying — it can be like trudging through mud with loose-fitting galoshes, especially for beginners. Even so, it's not simply a matter of the will. The *Catechism* says that we must "also learn how to pray" (2650).

In addition to the different types or forms of prayer — petition, adoration, thanksgiving, and so forth — there are three specific expressions, or stages, of prayer that are universal: vocal, meditative, and contemplative. They constitute a framework in which the forms of prayer operate. They also represent a ladder or progression in the life of prayer as you move into deeper and closer communion with God.

But keep this foundational point in mind: prayer has a goal — it's ordered to our perfection. It's one of the main ways we get our faces on one of those laminated holy cards. Of course, bookmark status takes time. There are many steps along the way as we are perfected. This life is more a marathon than a sprint. Perfection doesn't happen overnight.

And don't fool yourself into thinking that these types and stages of prayer are only for super-holy people and saints. It's actually the reverse. People become super-holy and saints precisely because of this kind of prayer life.

Couched in Prayer

Prayer is a kind of stairway to heaven (yeah, yeah, I know the song) by which we ascend toward God. As we climb toward him, the way we pray changes or matures.

Our prayer life plays out in some ways like the relationship of a couple who have been married for years and years. When they first fell in love, they constantly proclaimed their love to each other. This was typically followed by short bursts of smiling, giggling, and canoodling (I hate that word!) — all the activities aimed at disgusting an eight-year-old boy. When rational thought finally prevailed and the giggling died down, they'd spend hours talking about all kinds of things.

But as time went by, the mode of communication changed because the relationship had grown deeper. In fact, they didn't have to actually talk to communicate. For a couple married a long time, one grunt combined with an outstretched hand means, "Can you bring me a beer?" A roll of the eyes and silence while she flips to the next page of her magazine means, "You've been sitting on the couch all day. Get it yourself. You could use the exercise."

Now I am certainly not saying that the longer you're married, the less you should talk.

Ain't no way! I've been married more than a dozen years, but I learned pretty quickly that my wife never grows tired of my telling her how beautiful she is and how much I love her. My recommendation to all husbands is that you should say this sort of thing about every thirteen seconds.

My point is that, if you're a husband, as time goes by your wife doesn't need to talk to make you weak in the knees, either in a good way or in a bad way. On the one hand, you might shudder because she gives you the raised-eyebrow-with-head-slightly-tilted-down look, and you think, "What did I do?" On the other hand, perhaps you get a playful smirk, notice a little hand gesture, or simply look into her eyes and know what she's thinking. Why? Because you've spent so much time together that your relationship has grown and deepened. You are more united.

It's similar in your communication with God. You continue to engage in the different types and stages of prayer, but the way you do it changes as your relationship deepens.

Now before I get myself into any more trouble with wives around the world, let's move more specifically into these different expressions or stages of prayer and learn how we go about them.

Loud and Proud

The first stage of any prayer life is vocal prayer. "Lord, open my lips; my mouth will proclaim your praise," says the Psalmist (51:17, NAB). We're familiar and comfortable with this type of prayer, having been taught the Rosary, grace before meals, and similar vocal prayers from the time we were little. Jesus himself taught us the most famous vocal prayer, the Our Father. The Church supplies a storehouse of other vocal prayers such as the Liturgy of the Hours — that is, morning, midday, evening, and night prayer — prayers to the saints, Acts of Contrition, and so forth. We have a slew of beautiful prayers at our disposal.

Vocal prayer is important because we aren't simply spiritual beings. We are a union of body and soul, body and spirit, and so we need to translate our feelings externally. When my father-in-law watches his beloved Dallas Cowboys score a touchdown, he hoots and hollers with great satisfaction. When they mess up, he's never at a loss to describe their inadequacies in a highly colorful and emotional way. Why? Because human beings are designed to show emotion. We tend to act out what we're feeling. This translates into the way we worship. We raise our hands in worship. We kneel when we pray. We bow before receiving the Eucharist.

In other words, vocal prayer expresses our inner feelings and inner life. We don't leave vocal prayer behind as we progress in the life of prayer. In fact, the *Catechism* says it is "an essential element of the Christian life" (2701).

One reason it's essential is that our prayer lives aren't only personal. We are a family, and vocal prayer is necessary during those many times we pray together. Imagine if you were at Mass or some other gathering and the priest said, "Let us pray," and we all just stood there praying silently. Then twenty seconds later the priest said "Amen." "No, wait, Father. I wasn't finished!" It would be chaos. (I really wanted to say "Mass confusion," but I refrained.)

Vocal prayer always remains necessary for individual and group prayer, but you'll notice that as you spend more time alone with the Lord, your personal prayer will evolve and incorporate more silence.

Listen Up

Nevertheless, even when alone with God, we tend to talk too much. Saint John Chrysostom's admonition hits home: "Whether or not our prayer is heard depends not on the number of words, but on the fervor of our souls (St. John Chrysostom, *Ecloga de oratione* 2: PG 62, 585)" (CCC 2700). His point? When we engage in vocal prayer we must focus on what we're saying. Saint Teresa of Avila and Saint Francis de Sales confirm that, saying that one fervent Our Father or Hail Mary is far more effective than blowing through a Rosary with little concentration. Even Jesus said, "Do not heap up empty phrases" (Mt 6:7).

And though it's normally the first stage, vocal prayer isn't completely its own category of prayer. It can even become meditative prayer when we are focused on, and drawn into, the Lord. Think about the Rosary or the Stations of the Cross, for example. When you are really pondering what you are saying, you are in a sense meditating on the mysteries of God. This is why quality is better than quantity. You don't want to yap, yap, yap too much — it gets in the way of your growth. After all, what can you learn about someone if all you ever do is talk and never listen? As Mark Twain sagely observed, "If we were meant to talk more than listen, we would have two mouths and one ear." This leads us to our second type, or stage, of prayer: mental prayer, or meditation.

The Mystery of Meditation

The word "meditation" might bring to mind a certain image — such as a guy who dresses like Shaggy from Scooby Doo and sits in the lotus position. Perhaps his middle finger is making a circle with his thumb and he's chanting "ohm, ohm." (He's a hippie electrician.) But that's not what I'm talking about. That's not Christian meditation; that's more along the lines of Hinduism or Buddhism.

So what, exactly, is Catholic meditative, or mental, prayer? Essentially, it is attentive reflection on the Lord that is aided by spiritual input. It is interior prayer. And it is so important that Saint Alphonsus Liguori declared, "Short of a miracle, a man who does not practice mental prayer will end up in mortal sin."[68] I'll wait a moment so you can read that again. Why would St. Alphonsus make such a strong statement?

The *Catechism* sheds some light, telling us that real meditative prayer is a quest. It's where the "mind seeks to understand the why and how of the Christian life, in order to adhere and respond to what the Lord is asking" (2705). In other words, meditation is where we ponder the mysteries of Christ as he speaks to us in various ways so that our relationship with him grows. Put simply, meditative prayer is the way we grow in Christ. That's why it's so important.

And how does he speak to us? How does he reveal himself to us? If your first thought is through the Internet or television, I want you to put this book down and go run a lap.

Probably the most obvious way Christ speaks to us is through sacred Scripture, which is, after all, the Word of God. Lectio divina — reading and meditating on Scripture — is one of the most popular forms of meditative prayer. Or God might reveal himself through the lives of the saints, the beauties of nature, the liturgy, or any number of ways. All of these provide material for meditation upon him.

But we don't just think about God passively when we meditate. We aren't emptying our minds as in Eastern religions. To the contrary, meditative prayer is interactive. We ponder the mysteries of Christ and start an inner conversation with God. This is where we begin to become more intimate with God as we focus on him and let him seep into our being.

We're not just chatting, either. Every prayer is meant to bring about concrete action and resolutions in our lives so that we become more like God. The goal is for us to regain our likeness to him. Prayer is the means to achieve that goal.

But what does meditative prayer look like? The focus or center of meditative prayer is always Christ. Jesus himself tells us that he is the "the way, and the truth, and the life" and "no one comes to the Father, but by me" (Jn 14:6). He is the Word made flesh. He is God become man. We focus on the details of his life so that we can become more like him. This is why people emphasize meditation on the four Gospels. The Gospels are powerful because they're specifically about Christ's life.

Another quick point before we jump into the "how to" discussion: Christ is not only the center of our prayer, but also our chief role model. As he "humbled himself" to the point of death, we must seek humility, for it is the key to prayer (Phil 2:8). As the Book of Sirach says, "the prayer of the humble pierces the clouds" (35:17).

Practically Speaking

Now that we've considered the basics, how do we actually meditate? Here's a quick "how to" list that we'll build on going forward.

1. Pick location and time.
2. Recollect yourself.
3. Meditate.
4. Respond.
5. Resolve.

Since "PRMRR" is pure gibberish and fails miserably as an acronym, you're just going to have to reference the book or flat out memorize the list. Those are the breaks, kid.

Chaos Theory

Location and time are key factors in forming good prayer habits. You'll need to find a quiet place and decide on a time that works well for you. We're body-and-soul beings, and the physical aspects of prayer must work hand in hand with the spiritual side of things.

Of course, everyone's situation is different. Because of their state in life, some people won't have much quiet or free time. Our four kids consume a great deal of my wife's day while I'm at work. Whether it's driving to school, violin lessons, ballet, or simply chasing the rug rats around the house all day, her life can be chaotic and offer little time for repose. The only semi-regular time she has to pray is in the late evening or when the baby is napping. God understands. He's the consummate family man. But one way or another, do your best to have a set time to pray and try to stick to it.

Echoing Saint Paul, who urged us to "pray constantly," Saint Gregory of Nazianzus said, "We must remember God more often than we draw breath (St. Gregory of Nazianzus, *Orat. theo.*, 27,1,4: PG 36,16)" (CCC 2697). Sounds a little tough, huh? Paul and Gregory don't mean that we should go around constantly muttering prayers under our breath. Rather, they mean that even when we're not actively engaged in prayer, we are to live in a spirit of prayer that envelops all aspects of our life.

And we can't hope to do that unless we start by setting aside specific, special times to pray. If you don't make prayer a daily priority and a nonnegotiable item on your schedule, it will be the first thing that gets dropped from your to-do list when things get busy. (And when was your last non-busy day?) So set a workable time, and find a quiet place. (Hint: The bar down the street on Monday night at 7:30 when the game is on the giant flat-screen isn't a workable, quiet option.)

Even if you have the ideal place and time, entering into meditation isn't necessarily simple. Easily distracted, most of us are like little children when it comes to prayer. In fact, many of us would rather dig a ditch than be alone with the Lord for fifteen minutes.

It's pretty much a given that it's easier for us to find quiet than to actually *be* quiet. Which is, again, another reason why finding a quiet location is so important. The Desert Fathers didn't get their name from hanging out in the crowds. These masters of prayer wanted to get rid of any and all distractions.

Of course, the Desert Fathers were simply imitating Jesus. He would get up in the wee hours of the morning or stay up all night in order to have his alone time with his Father (see Mk 1:35; Lk 5:16). He even went by himself into the wilderness for forty days to talk to his dad. While this may work for extremely motivated readers who don't mind the lack of heating, cooling, and running water, it's not an option for most of us. Perhaps a better alternative is a church or an adoration chapel where you can literally be with Christ. It doesn't get any better than that.

Your Fifteen Minutes of Pain

The length of time to set aside will change as your prayer life develops. If you're new to meditative prayer, don't try to do too much too fast. Set aside ten to fifteen minutes a day for mental prayer. For most beginners, ten or fifteen minutes can feel like watching grass grow or paint dry. You keep looking at the clock. (Somebody grab me a shovel; I need to find a ditch.)

The more you pray, however, the more quickly time starts to fly by. After you've been practicing the art of meditation for a while, you'll find that an hour is gone before you know it. If you're skeptical, I don't blame you. I was, too, but I've experienced this phenomenon many times. It serves in a way as evidence that we were made for this type of communing with God. He's not going to force us, however. God completely respects our freedom. Like any true relationship, we have to make an act of the will and voluntarily enter into prayer with him.

Once you've settled into your prayer place and the sweet sound of silence rings in your ears, the next step is to recollect yourself. Put yourself in the moment by casting aside all the cares of the day so that you can focus on Our Lord.

One practical way to do this is by slowly and quietly repeating the name of Jesus or a brief prayer that you know. Eastern Orthodox Christians and many Catholics practice an ancient technique called the Jesus Prayer. Based on the story of the blind beggar in the Gospel of Luke, the prayer consists of repeating the beggars request, "Jesus, Son of David, have mercy on me!" (Lk 18:38).[69]

Reading a Scripture passage about Our Lord's passion can also help you enter meditative prayer. Whatever you do, the goal is to make yourself aware that you are in the presence of God.

Quality Not Quantity

Now you're ready to meditate. Pick up your Bible, spiritual reading, image, or whatever you're going to meditate upon, and begin.

As you do your spiritual reading, move through the material in a meditative manner. It's about quality, not quantity. Focus on it. Soak in it as in a long bubble bath. Don't rush. Don't rip through a bunch of pages in one prayer session. This isn't a race; it's prayer that lasts a lifetime. That being said, you don't have to stay with the material if there's simply nothing there for you. If you find yourself unmoved by a particular reading, keep going. At some point you will encounter material that brings an interior response.

I recommend books for use in meditative prayer on my website (www.MatthewSLeonard.com), but here's one you can start with right now. One of my all-time favorites (and the favorite of many saints) is *The Imitation of Christ*, the classic work by Thomas à Kempis. He was a spiritual master, and this little book is broken into short meditations that make it perfect for this exercise. I even have a version of it on my phone that I downloaded for free. If you can make it through two pages of that book without being convicted about something, then you're a better man than I. (If you're a woman, you're already better than I am. Yes, I'm pandering.)

Respond with Resolve

By reading, pondering, and applying what you read, you prepare yourself for what the great prayer warrior Father Thomas Dubay called the heart of Christian meditation: "adoring, praising, thanking, and sorrowing with inner, quiet words." In other words, he said, "these affections of the will and heart are the chief aim of meditation."[70]

These affections move you to respond to what you've meditated on, to apply your meditation to your own life, and to converse with the Lord about it. Pray for the grace to work on areas in which you feel convicted. Pray for virtue that will help you overcome the vices in your life that meditation brings to mind. Remember that this is about becoming more like Christ — when he reveals an area as deficient, you want to resolve to work on it.

Remember, too, that meditation is not intellectual study. You're not prepping for an exam. The point is relationship with God your Father and Jesus your brother through the Holy Spirit. You're with family. When Jesus prayed, he called his Father "Abba," which is an Aramaic word that translates literally into English as "Daddy."

Jesus is the Son of God, and he speaks to his Father in very familiar terms, as we'd expect. But we, too, are "sons in the Son" through our baptism into Christ's Mystical Body, so we can call Almighty God our Daddy as well.[71] Keeping that in mind will help you to relax about the details of meditation. God actually wants this to happen more than you do.

One final note. As you grow in prayer, you'll learn to allow the conversation to go the way the Lord moves it. You don't always have to do the same routine if you feel led otherwise. There may be times when you have a distinct urge to put down what you're reading or lay aside your rosary and simply gaze upon the Blessed Sacrament if you're in an adoration chapel, or simply close your eyes and think of God if you're somewhere else. In fact, this may be a sign that you are perhaps in a transition stage between meditation and contemplation.

The Gift of Contemplation

Let's take a look at the third, and in a sense highest, stage of prayer — contemplation. Don't confuse Christian contemplation with oriental mysticism or self-awareness techniques. Rather, it's a loving communion with God, where he is conforming us to his likeness (CCC 2713). Saint Teresa of Avila describes contemplation as "nothing else than a close sharing between friends."[72] We could call it a deep awareness of God's presence.

In meditative prayer you are thinking, reading, reflecting, and talking inwardly with God. In other words, you're doing something. You're taking initiative. But infused contemplation is different.[73] It comes from God; it's "given" by him. It's a gift. You can't produce it. That's what the term "infused" means. It comes from the Latin *infudere*, which means "to pour in," or *infusum*, "that which is poured in." We can't make contemplation happen, we merely receive it.

But while contemplation is a gift, we do play a role. Our job is to prepare the way for it. God gives to those who desire him, and though we can't control when and how he gives this gift, we can demonstrate our desire by preparing ourselves to receive it. It's like cleaning the house for company even though you don't know when they're going to arrive.

How do we do this? How do we prepare? Through other kinds of prayer, particularly meditation, and by practicing virtue. In so doing, we're acting like a small child who reaches up to his daddy asking to be picked up. Our Father in heaven, who wants to give us every good gift, eventually scoops us up in his arms and communes with us in an ever more powerful way.

Of course, as glorious as it all sounds, there's no doubt that achieving this type of union with God isn't easy. Even when a soul makes it into the first stages of contemplation (for there are multiple levels of each stage of prayer), it will probably still experience distractions. It happens even to the best of us (so I'm told). But as we continue to live the gospel life of prayer and virtue, God gives us more and more of himself. And, ultimately, that's what we're after: more God. He becomes more a part of us, and we of him. This is what we were made for!

Prayerful Puberty

While it's what we're made for, prayerful union with God doesn't happen overnight. It's a lifelong process akin to natural maturation which, as I recall, was sometimes a bit rough.

I wasn't very big when I was a young teenager. The only person I ever felt tall around was my mom, and she was descended from elves. Even so, my voice was like a foghorn. When I spoke, children trembled and small animals ran for cover. But my vocal move from piccolo to tuba wasn't as smooth as a slide trombone.

Unfortunately for me and the people in the next fairway, I once sliced a golf ball while accompanied by my older brothers on a family outing. As I yelled, "fore!" my voice cracked terribly. The memory of my brother's incessant laughter sometimes haunts me in the wee hours of the night. Alas, that was just the beginning. It took a while for the parts of my bodily symphony to play in tune.

Just as in puberty, in prayer you generally don't move quickly from one stage to another. And just as in adolescence, there are often miscues along the way. But don't sweat it. Growth in prayer takes time, as in the rest of your life.

Reading the Signs

While the transition between meditative and contemplative prayer is typically gradual, there are some indicators. As previously noted, you might feel an inclination during meditation to put down your reading material and leave thinking aside. You begin to experience a desire to simply be with Our Lord in a wordless way like the Psalmist who says, "Be still, and know that I am God" (46:10).

Be that as it may, it's difficult to put your finger on a hard definition of contemplation. It can't be described in a completely satisfactory or scientific manner. It's not feelings or words, nor is it images. It might overflow into your emotions, but it isn't essentially an emotional experience. Catholic mystics Saint John of the Cross and Saint Teresa of Avila use words such as "fragrance" and "warmth" to describe it, but they stress that it isn't necessarily a sensory experience.[74]

Contemplation happens on a deeper, spiritual level than our senses or emotions. It supersedes them. For this reason you see Saint John of the Cross mysteriously refer to it as a "dark" knowledge, because it doesn't fit into human conceptions.[75] Even so, there's often a deep peace, delight, and longing in contemplative prayer as God communicates himself to us.

Contemplation Is for All

Perhaps right now you're thinking, "This kind of prayer is all well and good for saints like John and Teresa, but it's impossible for me. I drink cheap beer. I like to go ice fishing. In fact, I think the term 'Sunday best' refers to my favorite football jersey. This deep prayer stuff can't be for regular people like me."

My friends, that couldn't be further from the truth. Even the highest levels of contemplation are not something set aside for only a few elite individuals. It's what every Catholic is called to.

The *Catechism* recounts an illuminating encounter between a holy peasant in Ars and Saint John Vianney. The Curé often saw him sitting in front of the tabernacle and asked the man what he was doing. "I look at him and he looks at me," replied the peasant (see 2715). That's about as good a definition as we're going to get of contemplation. And it didn't come from some highbrow theologian. It came from an ordinary, blue-collar guy who simply sat in the presence of God.

Rather than being extraordinary, contemplative prayer is the normal, ordinary development of our prayer life. Remember, the final goal of life is union with God. So it makes complete sense that our move toward union with him starts now. The stages of prayer aren't for later. Nothing that draws us closer to God is for "later."

But don't forget, as noted, prayer is not primarily an emotional experience. God often gives consolations and pleasant feelings to beginners, and these feelings are often misinterpreted as synonymous with growth. Just because you felt really good during and after your Rosary doesn't mean you're suddenly a spiritual giant.

But don't get me wrong. Delight in prayer is a good thing and certainly comes from God. Even so, prayer isn't rooted in emotion. In fact, you'll notice as you progress that there will be some very dry, seemingly barren times. This is part of the natural progression as God leads you to seek him no matter what you feel.

Dark Nights

When the cause for Mother Teresa's sainthood got underway and many of her writings became public, people were shocked to learn of the tremendous suffering and desolation she experienced, something that, until then, no one had suspected. She very much felt the presence of God in her early years, but she felt abandoned by him as time went by. For the last forty years of her life she struggled heroically with what Saint John of the Cross refers to as the "dark night of the soul," a feeling of abandonment by God often encountered by people who have reached the higher stages of prayer.

The "dark night of the soul" is the final purging process in prayer in which we learn to seek God no matter how distant he seems. What's unusual about Mother Teresa's case is that it lasted so long. Her fidelity to the Lord in spite of this is a testimony to the depth of her faith.

The true test of growth in prayer is how you are living, not your feelings. Jesus says, "You will know them by their fruits" (Mt 7:20). If you notice yourself being more humble, more patient, more loving, more pure — more like Christ — then you're growing in prayer and you're drawing closer to God. It's an ever-tightening circle because these virtues act like magnets — they're naturally attracted to God and pull you in his direction.

Hearing Things

An overemphasis on feelings is one error people often make, but another danger is that of mistaking your own preferences or desires for the voice of God. I'm not pointing fingers, but have you noticed that people can have odd notions regarding what they think God has told them? I recall a televangelist in the late 1980s who declared that God would take him "home" (sometimes translated as "die") if he didn't raise $8 million for medical scholarships at his university. He ended up raising the money, as well as the ire of a lot of people when shortly thereafter the entire medical school and the high-rise hospital he had built closed. (No surprise, given there were already five other hospitals in a city of 360,000 people.) The televangelist explained to an incredulous world that God told him the mission of the enterprise paralleled the brief but powerful public ministry of Christ.

We have to be careful not to confuse our own wants

with those of the Holy Spirit. If you think you're being told to do something that seems a bit odd, bounce it off someone you trust, either your spiritual director, if you have one, or your priest, or another spiritually mature person. Let someone tested in the spiritual life help you judge what's going on.

I Believe I Can Fly

But then there are those saints who actually do experience unusual supernatural phenomena or direction through their prayerful union with the Almighty. For example, both Saint Francis of Assisi and Saint Padre Pio received on their bodies the stigmata, the physical wounds of Christ corresponding to the wounds of his passion and crucifixion.

Saint Teresa of Avila actually had to be held down during a liturgy because she became so rapt, so engrossed in God, that she literally started to float away. Her fellow sisters grabbed her because they didn't want the rest of the congregation to freak out.

Floating nuns are impressive, and the wounds of Christ even more so, but the power of those in deep union with God sometimes plays out in more unusual ways as well. (As if a levitating woman is usual.) In other words, saints who have achieved the highest degrees of contemplative union with God have exhibited pretty amazing power even when they're not directly participating in the liturgy or deep in prayer. Because they're constantly in

God's presence his power can manifest itself even in odd circumstances — like facing down wild beasts who can rip out your throat.

Hungry Like the Wolf

Anybody who knows anything about anything knows that Saint Francis of Assisi loved animals. He's the patron saint of all animals (unlike Saint Felix of Nola, who just got spiders — nobody prays to that guy in my house). One story about Francis involves a wolf. And this wasn't just any wolf. This was a big, bad, terrible wolf. Far scarier than the beast little Peter faced (though I must confess to childhood nightmares related to *Peter and the Wolf*). But the people of the Italian town of Gubbio were far more terrified of this creature than I was of a Russian-themed cartoon. It seems that the wolf was constantly attacking man, woman, and animal; and it got to the point where nobody wanted to go outside the city walls.

Saint Francis had compassion on the people, and in a move reminiscent of Crocodile Hunter Steve Irwin, he decided to have a conversation with the brute. (As previously noted, confidence was never an issue for our Poverello.) He marched out of town heading to the wolf's hangout, which probably looked a little like the Bone Church. Upon seeing Francis, the wolf immediately had carnivorous designs upon his flesh, but Saint Francis made the Sign of the Cross and ordered the wolf to stand down, which he did. For all we know, he might even have persuaded the wolf to roll over and shake hands.

According to the story, Francis called him out: "Brother wolf, thou hast done much evil in this land, destroying and killing the creatures of God without his permission; yea, not animals only hast thou destroyed, but thou hast even dared to devour men, made after the image of God; for which thing thou art worthy of being hanged like a robber and a murderer." Saint Francis was no mincer of words.

Being the original wolf-whisperer, Saint Francis then brokered a deal between the townspeople and the now tamed critter. He recognized that the wolf was eating everyone because he was hungry, but if the people fed the wolf every day, the wolf must promise to stop killing them. This deal seemed to work for everyone, and legend has it that the wolf went door-to-door like a vacuum salesman for the next two years, receiving food from everyone. He became a kind of mascot who reminded the people of Saint Francis, and they mourned when the wolf finally died of old age.

Union Power

So, those in close union with God have displayed some amazing power — nuns have flown and wild animals have been tamed, to name just a couple of examples of the power of God in the lives of the saints. But while these stories make the headlines, more often than not God seems to move us in quieter ways as we grow closer to him. Perhaps you'll hear him ask you to speak to this person or that. Maybe you'll be moved to help someone you've never considered helping before. While I doubt he'll ask you to tame a wolf, he's always full of surprises, so be ready.

One way or another, as you feel him leading you, I encourage you to trust and do whatever he tells you. After all, you're being led by your Father, and this is a good thing. Correction: This is a great thing! Because when we're obediently attentive to God's will we're becoming more like him. And that's what it's all about.

CHAPTER 10

THE PERFECT ENDING

GOOD STORIES END THE WAY THEY'RE SUPPOSED TO. In fact, we could go so far as to say that good stories have a kind of destiny that is bound to unfold in a particular manner. The plot thickens until it "sets" into a finale that has to happen or it's just not right. Cinderella's prince must come. Jaws must die. Willy has to be free (even if he can't actually survive in the wild). Even if it's sad, a proper ending remains satisfying. We sorrowfully accept that this is the way it had to turn out — and then we go out for pizza.

On the other hand, we've all been to movies where we've walked away thinking, "That ending just didn't make sense." (*Planet of the Apes*, anyone?) I've watched people become angry because of final scenes that just don't work.

Of course, even knowing the inevitable ending doesn't keep us from being swept into a story. We often go to see movies even though we know what is going to happen before we even get to the theater. The guy gets the girl, the baddie gets what's coming, ET makes it home, and so on. We go see these movies over and over and over because they're satisfying.

All of this raises an interesting question. What is our "fitting" destiny? What is the ending to our epic story, the finale that makes sense of the human drama and satisfies our deepest longing? The obvious answer is "heaven," and we already spent a fair bit of time discussing it. But there's an aspect to our final destiny that isn't talked about much, and it might surprise you. It can be summed up in one word: "divinity." That's what it's all about. You and I are destined to be divinized.

Divine Dogma

As Catholics, we're quite used to throwing the word "grace" around. Original sin took away Adam's sanctifying grace. The sacraments restore us to grace. The Virgin Mary is "full of grace." We could go on. But what does that really mean? What does grace actually do?

I like the way the Eastern tradition of Catholicism answers that question. What the West calls the life of grace, the East calls "deification," or "divinization."[76] When you get down to it, divinization is essentially sainthood in its final form. We were made for the divine family of God, and we can't really, truly be part of that family unless we're really, truly like the rest of his family.

My in-laws have a dog named Dixie — and I use the term "dog" loosely. Dixie is an eight-pound (soaking wet) toy Manchester terrier that makes mice look menacing. She's the kind of dog that has to contemplate whether or not it's wise to leap off the couch because in her world two feet might as well be ten.

Even so, my mother-in-law loves this dog. In fact, she calls it her "furry little child." Be that as it may, when they go on vacation, Dixie has to go to the kennel, because regardless of the depth of the attachment between my in-laws and Dixie, she remains a dog (so to speak).

Now contrast that state of affairs with a family that adopts a baby, a real "furry little child." That little baby is incorporated into the family in a way a pet never can be because the baby shares the same human nature as the rest of the family even though it doesn't have the same bloodlines. It belongs in a human family because it is human.

But God takes this adoption thing even further. Jesus actually became human, "like his brethren in every respect," except sin (Heb 2:17). He joined humanity to his divinity in such a way that he is both fully God and fully man at the same time.[77] Even in heaven, he is all human and divine and always will be. Why did he do this? It's simple. He became like us so that we can be like him, true children of the Father.

Tunnel Vision

When talking about how we're saved from sin, it's common for Christians to view Christ as the bridge which spans the chasm between us and the Father that was created by sin. That's not wrong, but in reality Christ is more like the tunnel through which we must pass in order to be saved. Through the sacraments, we actually enter into the mysteries of Christ and become one with him (see CCC 1075).

Recall that beginning with baptism, we were incorporated into the Mystical Body of Christ. And in the sacrament of sacraments, the Eucharist, we partake of "a food capable of making man divine," says Saint Thomas Aquinas.[78] Therefore, as Saint Paul says, it is "no longer I who live, but Christ who lives within me" (Gal 2:20). Through the sacraments our divinization has begun.

Put simply, Jesus became man for the particular purpose of reopening the path to divine life. Adam was making his way down that path, but got lost and took us with him. The original "son of God" wasn't only booted out of the Garden, but out of the family (see Lk 3:38). He rejected his Father's wishes and so lost the life of grace. He lost his likeness to God.

The "New Adam," as Saint Paul calls Christ, came to restore us to that family, but in an even more powerful way. His Incarnation, death, and resurrection have opened the door for us to be like him in a way that Adam never was. It's for this reason, at the Easter Vigil, we hear, "O happy fault, O necessary sin of Adam which has gained for us so great a Redeemer." God has given us his own life. We literally become "partakers of the divine nature," declares Saint Peter (2 Pt 1:4).

Let the Children Come

Being in a state of grace ultimately means that we have rejoined the family of God. Don't forget that in order to enter the kingdom of God, Jesus said we must become "little children." That wasn't simply a figure of speech. The final goal is for you and me to become God's real children. And we're not simply talking about a legal decision where a judge approves a child's new last name; it's a divine adoption. We literally become "sons in the Son," children of God in a very real sense.[79] As Saint John the Evangelist proclaims, "See what love the Father has given us, that we should be called children of God; and so we are" (1 Jn 3:1).

But let's be clear about this. We don't become equal to God or get somehow swallowed up into him so that we lose our personhood. Rather, we become *like* him. He shares himself with us so that we can become by grace what he is by his very nature — divine! "God became man so that man might become God," declared Saint Athanasius. We don't become eternal, omniscient, or omnipotent — but we share in his knowledge and power. This is his gift of love, his gift of self that he freely bestows upon us. As author John Saward beautifully stated, "Christ in his heavenly beauty does not shine alone."[80]

And Christ calls on us to shine his love upon others as well. That's the core message of the New Evangelization. Love God and love neighbor with the love of God. It's not easy, I know. And when I find myself treating someone poorly or not loving enough, I'm haunted by the words of C. S. Lewis, who reminds us that divinity is the created destiny for every person we meet: "It is a serious thing to live in a society of possible gods and goddesses, to remember that the dullest and most uninteresting person you talk to may one day be a creature which, if you saw it now, you would be strongly tempted to worship."[81]

Isn't this all amazing? Every person is created to be divine, to be a member of God's own family! The question becomes what will our response be to this unfathomable gift of our Father in heaven? It can be only this. We must strive to be worthy. We must strive for sainthood. The art of living begins now. Paraphrasing Saint Catherine of Siena, Blessed John Paul II declared that "if you are what you should be, you will set the whole world ablaze!"[82]

No Regrets (Remix)

Time is short. You don't want to get to the end of your life, whenever that may be, and regret that you didn't live the way you were supposed to. That you didn't love Jesus and others the way they deserve. That you didn't partake of the body and blood of Jesus often enough. That you didn't pray. That you didn't do everything you could to ensure your own salvation, and that of your spouse and kids. This is it. There are no second chances. Remember that "life holds only one tragedy, ultimately: not to have been a saint." Jesus is waiting for you to give it all to him so he can give it all to you. In fact, he's already offering you all the grace you need so that perfection isn't a pipe dream. It's our destiny, and it starts now.

Live a life of no regrets. Don't cut any corners. Dedicate yourself to the God who made you, loves you, and offers you a mind-blowing eternity with him. It's the offer of a lifetime — literally.

ENDNOTES

Chapter 1

[1] Mike Aquilina, *The Fathers of the Church: An Introduction to the First Christian Teachers* (Huntington, IN: Our Sunday Visitor, 2006), 194.

[2] Maurice Picquard, *A New Portrait of Saint Vincent de Paul*, *Vincentian Heritage Journal* 1, Issue 3, Article 3, 1-1-1982.

[3] Cardinal John J. Wright, *The Saints Always Belong to the Present*, (San Francisco: Ignatius, 1985), 71.

[4] Ibid., 181.

[5] *Evangelii Nuntiandi*, 21.

Chapter 2

[6] *Evangelii Nuntiandi*, 2.

[7] Joseph Cardinal Ratzinger, Address to Catechists and Religion Teachers, December 12, 2000.

[8] Pope Benedict XVI, Homily, First Vespers, Solemnity of the Holy Apostles Peter and Paul, St. Paul Outside the Walls, Rome, June 28, 2010.

[9] *Redemptoris Missio*, 2.

[10] *Evangelii Nuntiandi*, 21.

[11] Ibid., 41.

[12] *Christifideles Laici*, 16.

[13] Pietro Giacomo Bacci, *The Life of St. Philip Neri: Apostle of Rome, and Founder of the Congregation of the Oratory* Vol. 1 ed. Frederick Ignatius Antrobus (London: Kegan Paul, Trench Trubner and Co Ltd., 1902), 294.

Chapter 3

[14] Joseph Cardinal Ratzinger, Address to Catechists and Religion Teachers, December 12, 2000.

[15] Ibid.

[16] St. Thérèse of Lisieux, *The Story of a Soul* (Trabuco Canyon, CA: Source Books, 1993), X.

[17] Pope Benedict XVI, Homily, First Vespers, Solemnity of the Holy Apostles Peter and Paul, St. Paul Outside the Walls, Rome, June 28, 2010.

[18] John K. Ryan trans., *The Confessions of Saint Augustine* (New York: Image, 1960), 65.

[19] Ibid., 248.

[20] In his essay *The Weight of Glory,* C. S. Lewis says that "surely a man's hunger does prove that he comes of a race which repairs its body by eating and inhabits a world where eatable substances exist. In the same way, though I do not believe (I wish I did) that my desire for Paradise proves that I shall enjoy it, I think it a pretty good indication that such a thing exists and that some men will. A man may love a woman and not win her; but it would be very odd if the phenomenon called 'falling in love' occurred in a sexless world." (p 4).

[21] John K. Ryan trans., *The Confessions of Saint Augustine* (New York: Image, 1960), 43.

[22] Scott Hahn and Mike Aquilina, *Living the Mysteries* (Huntington, IN: Our Sunday Visitor, 2003), 19.

Chapter 4

[23] Joseph Cardinal Ratzinger, *The Spirit of the Liturgy* (San Francisco: Ignatius, 2000), 27.

[24] Blessed Columba Marmion, *Christ the Life of the Soul,* trans. Alan Bancroft (Bethesda: Zaccheus Press, 2005), 10.

[25] *Mulieris Dignitatem,* 7.

[26] *Gaudium et Spes,* 24.

[27] Scott Hahn ed. *Catholic Bible Dictionary* (New York: Doubleday, 2009), 396.

[28] Ann Ball, *Modern Saints: Their Lives and Faces* (Rockford, IL: TAN Books, 1983), 357.

Chapter 5

[29] Marquis de Sade and Maurice Lever, *Bibliothèque Sade: Voyage d'Italie* (Paris: Fayard, 1995), 106.

[30] Ibid.

[31] *Salvifici Doloris,* 30.

[32] St. Thérèse of Lisieux, *The Story of a Soul* (Trabuco Canyon, CA:

Source Books, 1973), 130.

33 St. John of the Cross, *The Collected Works of St. John of the Cross*, (Washington DC: ICS Publications, 1991), 137.

34 Karol Wojtyla, *Love and Responsibility*, trans. H. T. Willetts, (San Francisco: Ignatius, 1993), 98.

35 G. K. Chesterton, *St. Francis of Assisi* (Garden City, NY: Image Books, 1924), 51.

Chapter 6

36 C. S. Lewis, *Letters to Malcolm: Chiefly on Prayer*, (San Diego: Harcourt, 2002), 108-109.

37 C. S. Lewis, *The Weight of Glory* (New York: HarperCollins, 1949), 30.

38 Josef Pieper, *Divine Madness* (San Francisco: Ignatius, 1995), 48.

39 John Saward, *The Beauty of Holiness and the Holiness of Beauty* (San Francisco: Ignatius, 1997), 25.

40 Sheldon Vanauken, *A Severe Mercy* (San Francisco: Harper, 1977), 26.

41 C. S. Lewis, *The Weight of Glory* (New York: Harper Collins, 1949), 42.

42 Peter Kreeft, *Heaven: The Heart's Deepest Longing* (San Francisco: Ignatius, 1980), 78.

43 John Henry Newman, *Parochial and Plain Sermons* (San Francisco: Ignatius, 1997), 852.

44 Robert Wilken discusses this point in his excellent work *The Spirit of Early Christian Thought* (New Haven: Yale University Press, 2003), 273-274.

45 Servais Pinkaers said that Bossuet remarked this in *The Pursuit of Happiness — God's Way: Living the Beatitudes* (New York: St. Paul's, 1998), 25.

46 Ibid., 18.

Chapter 7

47 George William Rutler, *The Curé of D'Ars Today* (San Francisco: Ignatius, 1988), 81.

48 Ibid., 90.

49 Ibid., 82.

[50] Ibid., 87.

[51] Ibid., 183.

[52] Scott Hahn and Mike Aquilina, *Living the Mysteries: A Guide for Unfinished Christians* (Huntington, IN: Our Sunday Visitor, 2003), 161.

[53] *Sacrosanctum Concilium*, 10.

[54] Ignatius of Antioch, *Letter to the Ephesians*, 20:2.

[55] *Lumen Gentium*, 11 (cf. CCC 1324).

[56] Blessed John Paul II, General Audience, June 21, 2000.

[57] Mike Aquilina, *Fire of God's Love: 120 Reflections on the Eucharist* (Cincinnati: Franciscan Media, 2009), 2.

Chapter 8

[58] For a deeper discussion of the heavenly nature of the Mass, read Scott Hahn's *The Lamb's Supper* (New York: Doubleday, 1999).

[59] *Explanations of the Psalms*, 33:1:10.

[60] *Verbum Domini*, 55.

[61] Baltimore Catechism 1 Q6 asks, "Why did God make you?" The answer is "God made me to know Him, to love Him, and to serve Him in this world, and to be happy with Him for ever in heaven."

[62] José María Escrivá de Balaguer, *The Forge* (Manila: Sinag-Tala, 1988), 762.

[63] G. T. Stupart, trans., *Library of the Fathers of the Holy Catholic Church* (London: J. H. Parker), 273.

[64] Augustine, *Confessions* (London: Penguin, 1961), 177.

[65] Ibid.

[66] A great introduction to Scripture is Scott Hahn's *A Father Who Keeps His Promises* (Cincinnati: Servant, 1998).

[67] *Manual of Indulgences* (Washington, DC: USCCB, 2006), 100.

Chapter 9

[68] Dom Jean-Baptiste Chautard, *Soul of the Apostolate* (Garden City, NY: Image, 1961), 91.

[69] Anthony M. Coniaris, *Philokalia* (Minneapolis: Light and Life Publishing, 1998), 42-52.

[70] Fr. Thomas Dubay, *Prayer Primer* (Cincinnati: Servant, 2002), 75.

71 *Gaudium et Spes*, 22.

72 Saint Teresa of Jesus, *The Book of Her Life*, 8,5 in *The Collected Works of St. Teresa of Avila*, trans. K. Kavanaugh, OCD, and O. Rodriguez, OCD (Washington, DC: Institute of Carmelite Studies, 1976), I, 67; cf. CCC 2709.

73 Spiritual masters like St. John of the Cross and St. Teresa of Avila discuss different levels within each of the three stages of prayer.

74 See *The Fire Within*, by Fr. Thomas Dubay (San Francisco: Ignatius, 1989), 59.

75 Kieren Kavanaugh, OCD and Otilio Rodriguez, OCD, trans., *The Collected Works of St. John of the Cross* (Washington, DC: ICS Publications), 629.

Chapter 10

76 The Eastern tradition also uses the word '*theosis*.' For a full discussion of this topic see *Deification and Grace* by Daniel Keating (Ave Maria, FL: Sapientia, 2007).

77 Theology professors with alphabets after their names refer to this as the "hypostatic union," which was formally defined at the Council of Ephesus way back in A.D. 431. The council said that after the Incarnation, Jesus is eternally both human and divine.

78 Daniel Keating, *Deification and Grace* (Ave Maria, FL: Sapientia Press, 2007), 45.

79 For a concise summary of divinization and Catholic spirituality in general, see Scott Hahn's essay titled "Come to the Father: The Fact at the Foundation of Catholic Spirituality" in *Four Views on Christian Spirituality* (Grand Rapids, MI: Zondervan, 2012), 73.

80 John Saward, *The Beauty of Holiness and the Holiness of Beauty* (San Francisco: Ignatius, 1997), 19.

81 C. S. Lewis, *The Weight of Glory* (New York: HarperCollins, 1980), 45.

82 John Paul II, Homily at the Closing of World Youth Day, *Tor Vergata*, August 2000.

About the Author

Matthew Leonard is an internationally-known speaker, author and Executive Director of the St. Paul Center for Biblical Theology. After serving as a missionary in Latin America, he earned his Master's degree in Theology from Franciscan University. Matthew and his wife Veronica have four children and make their home in Ohio. More information about Matthew can be found at www.MatthewSLeonard.com.